You and Your Freezer
Buying. Stocking. Using

Jess Mitchell

Hutchinson Benham, London

Contents

Hutchinson Benham Limited
3 Fitzroy Square, London W1

An imprint of the Hutchinson Group

London Melbourne Sydney Auckland
Wellington Johannesburg and agencies
throughout the world

First published 1976
Second (revised) edition 1977
© Jess Mitchell 1977

Set in Monotype Times

Printed in Great Britain by litho
by Hunt Barnard Web Offset Ltd
and bound by Wm Brendon & Son Ltd
of Tiptree, Essex

ISBN 0 09 126551 7

1. You and your freezer

'To freeze or not to freeze' – this is the question being asked and argued over by the still thousands of freezer-less families in Great Britain today. This topic is discussed with great enthusiasm by housewives and with even greater enthusiasm by their husbands, in the office, on the factory floor, the local, or wherever people gather together. No

longer is the freezer looked upon as a luxury item in the home, but as a necessity. In fact I would like to stick out my neck here and say *every* home should have one – *you really can't afford* to be without one. Many years ago ninety per cent of freezer owners lived in the country; *they* really appreciated the value of having a 'Supermarket' of their own – there was no High Street or corner shop for them and in winter they could be cut off for days. But today more and more people are becoming aware of the advantages of a food freezer, whether they live in suburbia, a new housing estate, or the tenth floor of a block of flats. We all have to eat – food shopping has to be done – and this all takes time; time that we can ill afford, and with so many housewives having full or part-time employment, every hour is valuable. By having a freezer you can, therefore:

1. Cut down on time spent shopping and the mental and physical wear and tear on your body.

2. Have more time to spend with your family – this is so important today. No one likes a moaner – you can't do this and that because you have the shopping to do or the meals to cook.
3. Have more time to enjoy hobbies, and what is *most important* of all, have more money in your purse.
4. Reduce the temptation of buying 'special offers' that you really don't need. How many of us are strong enough not to want to try some new product at a supposedly give-away price?

You don't really believe me, do you?

How much money do *you* spend each year on food? £800 or £900 perhaps. The amount naturally will depend very much on how many you have in your family, and how many meals are eaten each day at home, but, whatever your circumstances, as a freezer owner you can make a saving of at least twenty per cent on food bills – not to be sneezed at these days. Therefore, your freezer is an investment which will easily pay for itself within the first two years. Not only will this valuable piece of equipment save money for you, but as a long-term investment the returns are well above average – and tax free.

Your husband may be a keen gardener. How many times during the summer do you give away the surplus crop? With a freezer your own family can enjoy home grown vegetables and fruit from one growing season to another. Who knows, you might even encourage gardening rather than golf, football or cricket. Just think of the savings! He might also enjoy fishing and shooting, and if he has had a good catch or a good bag, put an end to playing Santa Claus, pop the fish or game in the freezer – let *your* family have the benefits, not the neighbours.

Being a freezer owner opens up a whole new world for every family; the advantages are tremendous, one being the personal satisfaction of knowing that you have a wide variety of food, not only for the family, but for the unexpected visitors as well. There is no need ever to be caught out with nothing in the cupboard or the refrigerator. You have the reassurance of knowing that all food is being preserved in the best possible way; after all, freezing is the most natural method of preserving food, with its flavour, colour, and – most important of all – its nutritional value unharmed.

When you have finally decided to buy a freezer you will have taken the biggest step in making your home complete, convenient and modern. You will come to rely on your freezer more and more, and will soon be saying to your friends, 'I don't know how I ever managed without it.'

In this book I do sincerely hope that I can help *you* to become a really happy freezer owner, confident in the knowledge that you have chosen the right freezer, purchased from a reliable company, with good after-sales service, and that your freezer management is geared to suit the needs of your family.

As a home economist and, perhaps more importantly, as a working wife who has been very much involved with freezers and food for many years, my advice and suggestions are based on practical experience. I'll try to help you avoid the pitfalls and disappointments which many of us experience in our early months of being freezer owners. I've talked to thousands of housewives and hundreds of husbands on this subject and through these pages I hope now to have the opportunity of helping *you* choose and use *your* freezer to advantage.

CHOOSING YOUR FREEZER

Finally making the decision to invest in a freezer is in most cases the easiest part of the operation. What type to buy and where to buy it can be very time-consuming, and I do hope that in this chapter I will be able to give you some help in making your final decision. There are basically three types of freezers to choose from – the chest freezer, the upright freezer and the fridge-freezer, and we will now take a close look at each type.

The chest freezer

Chest freezers are available in a wide range of sizes, from the small 4 cu. ft. (113 l.) Model to the very large 29 cu. ft. (821 l.) size, but whichever size you buy depends very much on how much space you have available, or how much use you are going to make of your freezer. Never buy too small – my advice is to buy the biggest that space and income will allow. Perhaps if I say that in each cubic foot of freezer space you can store up to 25 lbs. ($11\frac{1}{2}$ kg) weight of food, this will help you to decide which size you are going to have, but the most popular size range is between 9 and 14 cu. ft. (255 and 396 l.). The chest freezer has a top-opening, well-balanced and fully insulated lid, some with interior lights,

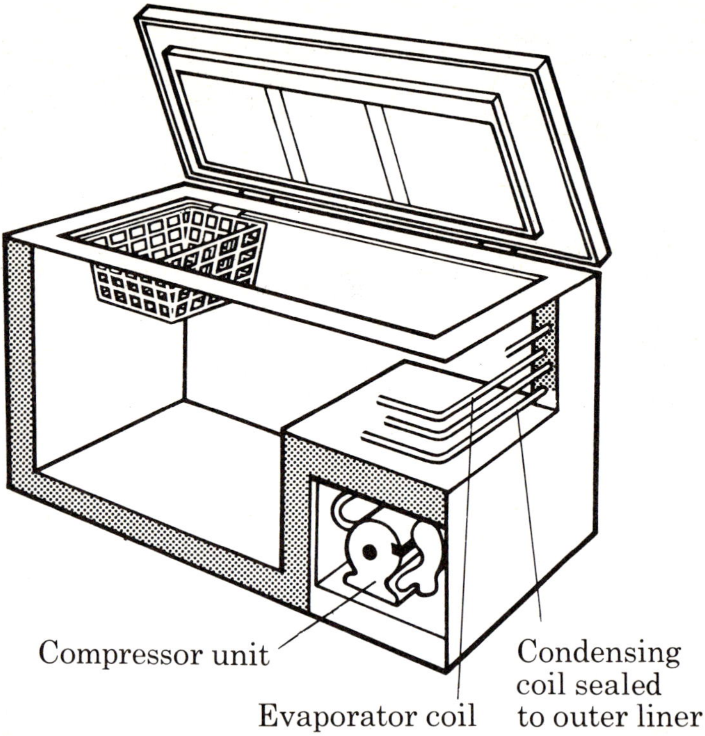

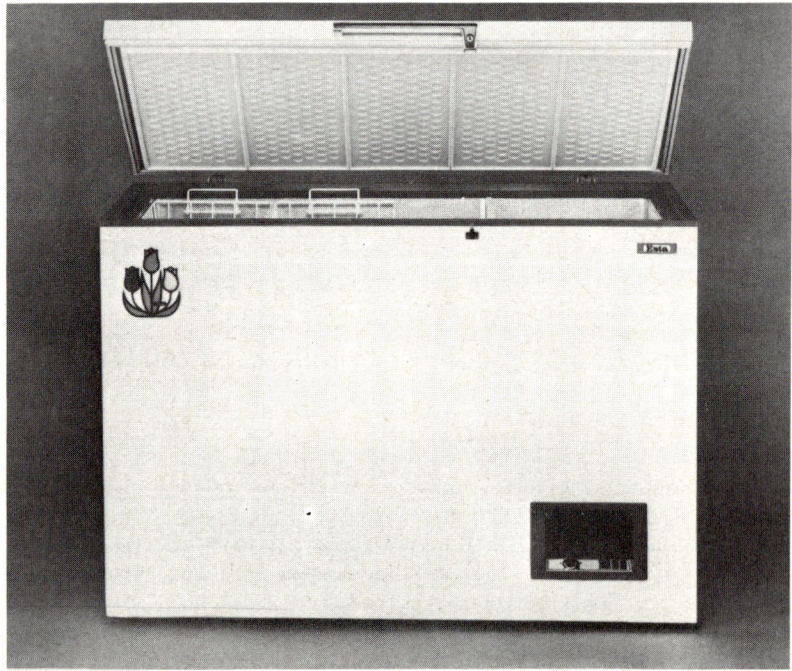

Compressor unit

Evaporator coil

Condensing coil sealed to outer liner

Nesso Coolflo 120 4.2 cu. ft chest freezer

and a fast freeze section for the freezing down of fresh food. Some makes, e.g. AEG and Beekay, have fast freeze sections with refrigeration on four walls and on the bottom, while others have refrigeration on only three walls. Most come complete with one, two or three baskets, depending on capacity, and in some cases plastic-coated space dividers. Extra

Opposite: Esta HF 421 chest freezer

baskets or dividers can always be bought separately. Kitchens in Great Britain are really, as yet, not designed to accommodate the large chest freezers, but if you haven't space in your kitchen, and your choice is to have a chest freezer, it will live quite happily in the garage, under the stairs. or, if you are absolutely stuck for space, the spare bedroom. This type is still the most popular, costs less to buy and running costs are slightly lower.

Check when buying that *you* can reach the bottom of the freezer. This can be a difficulty if you are small – you don't want to fall in!

The chest freezer either has a skin type condenser or a fan-cooled condenser; both are naturally recommended, but for the freezer which is going to spend its life in the garage I would strongly recommend to you the skin condenser, because with the fan cooled condenser type you would find condensation gathering on the metal surface, and this could in time cause rusting. Again, if the freezer is in the garage, leave it sitting on the wooden frame on which it was delivered, thus allowing good air circulation underneath to keep the base dry. There are times when the car is driven into the garage wet or with snow under the bumpers. I certainly don't dry my car down – I haven't got the time.

The upright freezer

This type is growing in popularity quite rapidly as it only takes up a small amount of floor space, usually the same as the average size domestic refrigerator. Once again there are many sizes to choose from. The smallest free-standing models, approximately 2 cu. ft. (57 l.) capacity, are designed

8

to stand on top of a refrigerator or on any working surface. The upright is front-opening with either one or two doors, depending on cubic capacity and design, and can have the doors opening to either left or right. They are easy to pack and you can see at a glance what is on each shelf or drawer. Once again, if you are small and have decided to buy a large capacity upright, you may have difficulty in reaching the top shelf – stools are not provided – so if this is the case use the top shelves for long-term storage. Beekay have designed – very cleverly I think – their 12 cu. ft. (340 1.) upright, with the unit on the top, therefore, if you are small you don't have the problem of over-stretching or climbing up on a not

AEG Arctis 26 GS and Arctis 400 GS Automatic upright freezers

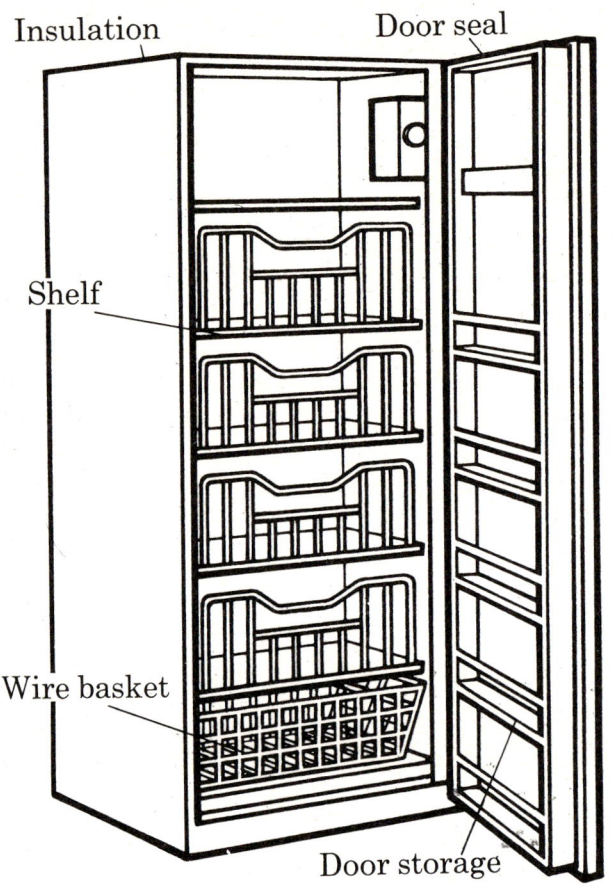

Insulation   Door seal

Shelf

Wire basket

Door storage

too safe kitchen stool. Many upright models have shelves on the door which you will find quite useful, particularly for small size packs, which seem to have a habit of disappearing in the freezer. Some models have a special fast freeze shelf, drawer or compartment, while in others any shelf can be used for fast freezing. The upright freezer is slightly more expensive to run, particularly those large single door models where the fall-out of cold air is considerable if the design does not include shelf doors which help to keep the cold inside the freezer. When choosing a large upright, say 12 cu. ft. plus, (340 1. +) buy one with two doors – use one half for long-term storage and the other for your daily needs. And remember, it is very important to make quite sure that the door or doors are very well fitting.

The fridge-freezer

Many manufacturers are now marketing this dual purpose piece of equipment. Most houses today have a refrigerator and in many instances

Tricity Deepcold Sovereign, 8.5 cu. ft refrigerator capacity side by side with a 7.3 cu. ft freezer cabinet

there is just no space available for a freezer, so to solve the problem the fridge-freezer has been designed. These come in a wide variety of sizes, but usually the cubic capacity of the refrigerator section is greater than that of the freezer section. This, from my own personal point of view, is the wrong way round. You always need more freezer space than refrigerator space – I would say the ideal combination is around 3–4 cu. ft. (85–113 1.) refrigerator and 8–10 cu. ft. (227–283 1.) freezer. In some cases a fridge-freezer is purchased for the kitchen while the housewife still keeps her chest freezer in the garage. When you become a freezer owner you never seem to have enough space, so this added capacity really does help. Many families perhaps needing to buy a new refrigerator haven't got a freezer, so a fridge-freezer might be their choice. I find that many couples in the older age bracket buy a fridge-freezer when their families have left home. Always remember that as you grow older the problems of shopping increase. You may not need to buy food in such large quantities but you still need to eat and you are not so able to shop – I know many housewives who don't become freezer owners until they are sixty or older. A freezer is not just for the young busy housewife.

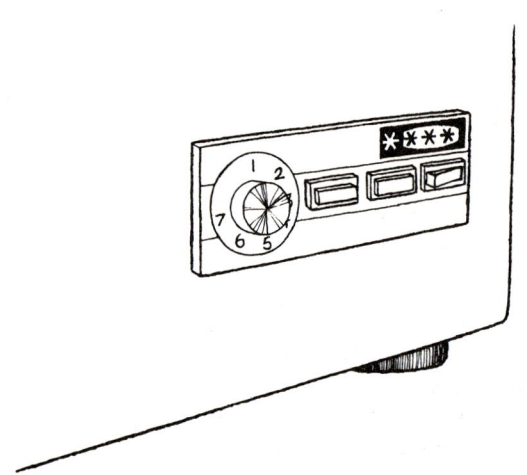

The freezer symbol

In the past there has been some confusion between a true freezer manufactured to freeze food efficiently, and a piece of equipment manufactured to conserve already frozen food. The freezer symbol (a six-pointed white star in front of the well-known three-star refrigerator sign) now makes it easy for you to know that you are buying a *food freezer* and not a *conservator*. Manufacturers who display this symbol on their models will state in the instructions their recommendations as to how much fresh food can be frozen as a single load in twenty-four hours. This is known as the daily freezing capacity.

WHERE TO BUY YOUR FREEZER

The final choice of freezer will naturally be yours, but perhaps I can save you some time, effort and discussion, and dare I say indecision, by making the following suggestion: one question I would like you to ask in *all* the freezer centres, shops and showrooms – Does the price quoted for the freezer include *delivery and installation?*

The widest range of freezers can usually be seen in freezer and food centres. Dewhurst, the well-known butchers, have now a chain of such shops – you already know their reputation as butchers and their freezer and food centres have the same high standard of quality and service. Bejam was the first company in Britain to offer this specialized service in freezers and frozen food to the housewife – they have a chain of shops where you will be given expert advice on freezers and food. They also have now a team of home economists specially trained to help you make the most of your freezer. The Co-op also have freezer and food shops up and down the country. Reputable companies such as these have well-trained staff who are really specialists in this field and they will offer a first class after sales service. You can cope for a few days if the washing machine breaks down, but you can't cope with a faulty freezer full of food. You must make quite certain that the after sales service guarantees to repair or replace your freezer within twenty-four hours. The Electricity Board showrooms throughout the country also have an above average selection of freezers – many boards have freezers manufactured for them under their own brand label, but also stock nationally known makes. One point to take into consideration here is that, if your husband's job is such that you move house fairly often, it is worth while remembering the Electricity Board is national, and whether you are in Land's End or John O' Groats, there will be a district office with stand-by staff to deal with emergencies.

Every departmental store and every large national electrical retailer has freezers to sell. Their prices are normally very competitive, but their selection is sometimes limited. Remember too that the staff in both electricity boards and large retail electrical department stores have so many pieces of equipment to sell that it is almost impossible for the staff to have specialized knowledge of every piece of equipment, but I did find in most of the larger stores that manufacturers' staff dealt with their own equipment very efficiently.

One must not overlook the small independent electrical retailer or the refrigeration engineer. You can see a variety of freezers – in some cases very limited – but the independent shopkeeper I find really does look after *you*, his customer.

Buying your freezer from a Cash & Carry

Freezer prices offered by Cash & Carry are generally lower than those offered by deep freeze centres. However it is worth exploring the facts before deciding whether it is worth paying less at a Cash & Carry. There

13

are two main points to look for. One is that if you buy from the Cash & Carry it means what it says! You have to transport the machine back to your home yourself. Because it has probably travelled from the other side of Europe, it is not unreasonable to expect that it could be marked or damaged. One is then faced with accepting an imperfect product or taking the machine back or trying to change it. Also the installation of the freezer can be a heavy and awkward process.

The other, bigger problem will be if the freezer goes wrong. You will probably be referred back to the manufacturer. This can be an ordeal with up to £100 worth of food at risk. May I strongly advise you to buy your freezer from a shop or freezer centre who will deliver and install for you. In addition, full after sales service will be available. Remember the old saying 'you only gets what you pays for'. As a freezer has a long life it is generally worth paying a little extra for full service even for the first year which is the most likely time when your freezer will go wrong.

To summarize briefly for you my findings: if you buy from a reputable company which is really interested in *you*, the customer, they will offer you first class service and advice. They will also undertake to do the following:

1. Put the freezer on a test run before delivery. There is nothing more infuriating than having a large piece of equipment delivered, just to find that it is faulty.
2. The freezer will be unpacked and placed in position with the plug top on. It won't just be dumped – perhaps on the front lawn – and then you will have to wait until your husband comes home before you can switch it on.
3. The delivery men will give you a few simple instructions just to get you started.
4. Guarantee a twenty-four hour breakdown service, seven days a week. You really do still find this type of service in Britain today.

Having now bought the freezer of your choice and had it delivered and placed in position, the next thing you must do before plugging in and switching on is to wash it out thoroughly, using a solution of warm water and bicarbonate of soda; then, before switching on, make sure that it is completely dry. Never use a soap or detergent solution inside the cabinet as there may be odours remaining which could be transferred to the food. Wash down the outside of the cabinet and, if necessary, use a spray polish to remove any marks.

You are now ready for the big 'SWITCH ON'. I would recommend that the freezer has a separate plug socket – don't, if it can be avoided, use a socket which you use for other appliances, as it is *so* easy to switch off. In fact, as a double safety precaution, when the freezer has been plugged in and switched on, cover the plug and switch with a piece of adhesive, cellotape or black tape. This will act as a protection against some member of the family accidentally switching off the supply. I also have a notice above the plug socket for my freezer which says '*DO NOT SWITCH OFF!*'. Remember please that, when you go off on holiday, you can no longer switch off the electricity at the mains. Oh yes, it happens many times, but you only make this mistake once. The disappointment of coming home to find all you food RUINED – need I say any more?

After switching on, your next thoughts must be – how and when am I going to fill it? Don't panic, take your time, for I reckon that most housewives find that their freezers will not be filled to capacity for at least six months, especially if they have bought the biggest freezer that space and finance will allow. Take into account too the growing season – if you buy your freezer in winter you have to wait until early summer to harvest your own fruit and vegetables. You may have purchased your freezer for a specific purpose, but let us now look at the wide variety of foods which can be stored.

As a guide to help you get started I would suggest that you allocate your freezer space as follows, bearing in mind that in each cubic foot (28 l.) of freezer space you can store 20–25 lbs. (10–12½ kg) weight of food.

30% Meat, poultry and game

30% Do-it-yourself freezing (fruit, vegetables, dairy produce, home baking, stock, soup, standby supplies of bread and rolls.

10% Commercially frozen vegetables and fruit. (This space allocation should be increased if you don't have home grown produce, or the time to prepare fruit and vegetables for freezing.)

10% Fish – this may be of the commercially frozen varieties. Fillets are most popular, either individually frozen, egged and crumbed or in batter, and these can be taken straight from the freezer and cooked. Don't forget the fish fingers and the fish cakes, but if your husband's hobby is fishing you will probably have to allocate more than 10% for his catch.

10% Ice cream, puddings and desserts.

10% Family meals. Meals or snacks for the unexpected guests.

There are only a few foods which don't freeze well:

Salad plants	— Lettuce, endive, chicory, cucumber – these turn limp, discoloured and watery.
	Tomatoes do freeze but can only be used for cooking.
Bananas	— turn black.
Single cream	— separates and mayonnaise curdles.
Hard boiled eggs	— whites become leathery.

Think about insurance – both food spoiling and maintenance.

FREEZER INSURANCE

Insurance is a good idea for two reasons. Firstly freezers can break down. A £65 bill for replacing a compressor – the motor of the freezer – is the sort of expense one can be faced with. Secondly if the freezer does, for any reason, stop working there is the loss of the contents. In the average 12 cu. ft. (340 1.) freezer this can be worth up to £100. How can you protect yourself against these possible expenses?

My advice is to play safe and take advantage of one of the insurance policies and freezer breakdown plans now available. Most of these plans represent good value and one of the best is the Nationwide Freezer Protection Plan. Other insurance schemes may require you to find the engineer in the first place and this can be a frustrating experience especially as time is of the essence. The Nationwide scheme however, provides engineers rapidly and, more important, pays the bill. Provided the freezer is less than ten years old you qualify for this scheme which gives automatic coverage against freezer breakdown.

RUNNING COSTS

The running cost of your freezer will be determined by:

1. The size, design and quality of the model which you buy.
2. The number of times that it is likely to be opened each day.
3. The length of time that the lid or door is left open.
4. The temperature of the kitchen, utility room or garage where the freezer is situated.
5. The temperature of fresh food when it is loaded into the freezer.

Most manufacturers will give an estimate of the number of units likely to be used by the various models which they produce, on their 'instructions for use' leaflet. On average the number of units of electricity used will be approximately between 1·75 to 2 units per cubic foot (28 1.) per week. The actual cost of running your freezer will relate to the basic unit charge for electricity in your area. A well stocked freezer is also much more economical to run than a half empty one, because no electricity is being wasted chilling the empty air space.

PACKAGING MATERIALS TO BUY TO GET YOU STARTED

All foods to be stored in the freezer must be carefully wrapped and sealed in polythene bags or containers which are *recommended for food freezing* – otherwise the food will lose its flavour and dry out. The results then will be most disappointing. If you use thin plastic bags they can so easily burst or tear. No housewife is very happy if the peas or sprouts have to be rescued from the bottom of the freezer. Other foods, e.g. meat, poultry, fish, may get *freezer burn* – this is the name given to the white or discoloured patches caused by drying out. This happens when the food has been exposed to the sub-zero temperatures of the freezer when the wrapping has been torn or the seal burst.

You don't have to spend a fortune on packaging materials. Most companies who sell freezers also have a good selection of packing materials to offer. Buy the basic essentials first – polythene bags with or without gussets, wire ties either paper- or plastic-covered, labels, a few plastic boxes with self-sealing lids, and a selection of foil plates and containers, a roll of heavy duty aluminium foil and a roll of plastic film.

Most housewives will already have a selection of Tupperware containers – make full use of them in your freezer. The square or oblong containers stack well and save freezer space, and a point worthy of note is that each piece carries a ten-year guarantee. Many of the Tupperware containers which I use in my own freezer are twelve years old now and still going strong.

Pack-n-Freeze Set

There is always something new from Tupperware – and their latest addition, at the time of going to press, is the Pack-n-Freeze Set above. This is a pack of ten containers in yellow and blue in three handy sizes: 0·5 litre, 0·85 litre and 1·4 litres, together with three sheets of special freezer labels in green, blue and red.

Thorpac Ltd

This company is one of Britain's leading specialist distributors of freezer packaging and accessories. Thorpac have a very extensive range of everything you need for food freezing. You will be able to see this range in many freezer centres, supermarkets, department stores and stationers, and for the new freezer owner I think that their Starter Pack is excellent (see illustration overleaf). This pack contains polythene bags

in assorted sizes, bag ties and labels, as well as polythene lined freezer bags which are ideal for freezing stewed fruit, soups, sauces etc. There is also a selection of foil plates and containers.

I was most interested too in a new product of Thorpac's – freezer layer tissue, which keeps food separated while freezing. It really is a must when freezing steaks, chops, hamburgers, chicken joints etc.

Remember you should always use packaging materials which are recommended for freezing. Packing is most important – buy *quality* not *quantity*. It's not worth saving pennies when preserving food in your freezer worth *pounds*.

If you enjoy doing what I call 'Fireside Shopping' why not drop a line to: Lakeland Plastics (Windermere) Ltd.,
    Alexandra Road,
    Windermere, Cumbria.

They will be pleased to send you their catalogue. This firm specialize in mail order and do have a wide range of packaging materials for you to choose from at leisure. They can offer a wide range of colour-coding accessories from tricolour bags to boxes with coloured lids. It's not often these days you can get free advice from experts, but you can from

Lakeland Plastics for they have a home freezing advisory service. Just write to them with your problem; they are always pleased to help out, and if you are a member of a club, they have a twenty-minute film entitled 'Freezeasy' on home freezer packaging which you would really enjoy seeing. Write to the Information Officer at Lakeland Plastics for details.

If you want to economize on packaging materials may I suggest the following items which you can use from your store cupboard: plastic containers with airtight lids, e.g. margarine cartons, honey cartons – these are ideal for short-term storage of small quantities, sauces,

New Thorpac freezer layer tissue (each sheet approximately 10″ x 15″) which comes in a 50-sheet pack

purée, fruit, trifles. Their lids have to be sealed – use the special freezer tape, normal tape will not withstand sub-zero temperatures; glass jars which have fairly straight sides and screw tops and coffee jars of varying sizes are excellent. We always have a selection of jars stored in some cupboard or other – they can be used over and over again. Use these for dry goods such as grated cheese, bread and cake crumbs, stock, soup, stewed fruit. But remember, when freezing liquid you must leave room for the liquid to expand – this is what we call head space – and you should only fill the jar to within $\frac{1}{2}''$–$1''$ (1–2 cm) from the top. If you don't feel too happy about freezing in jars, experiment – select a few jars, coffee, honey, jam etc., fill each three-quarters full of water, screw on the lids and wrap each one in a polythene bag – put them in the freezer for two days; if, after that time, they haven't cracked you can use these

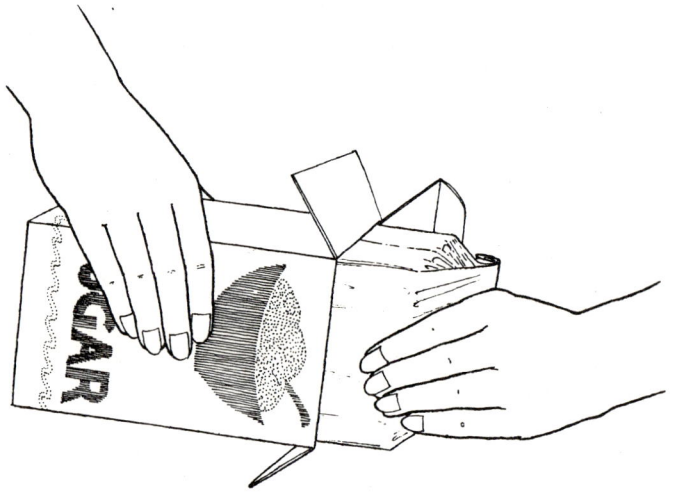

jars from the same brand of coffee, honey, jam etc., in the future. Sugar boxes or other square-cornered packets can be used as moulds – line with a polythene bag, pour in the food, e.g. stock, soup, stewed fruit, meat dishes, and freeze for twenty-four hours. Remove the bag, seal and label. Uniform packs such as these stack well and do save on valuable freezer space. Rigid plastic containers can also be used in the same way.

Ice cube trays are very useful for freezing parsley, mint, orange and lemon rind. Chop the parsley or mint, fill the ice cube tray and then pour over just enough water to hold together. When frozen remove from tray and store in polythene bags. Do the same with the orange and lemon rind. It is so useful to have these cubes for making sauces.

Nylon string shopping bags are most useful in the chest type freezer – you can pack together all vegetables of the one variety, bags of buns, bags of fruit etc. This does help to keep the freezer tidy.

Sealing and labelling of food packed in polythene bags

It is important to remove as much air as possible from the bag, because if you don't it can cause discolouration and will most certainly slow down the freezing process, and you will also find a white frost building up inside the bag. I remove the air by the most economical and simple method: place the food in the bag and gather the open end fairly tightly between your thumb and first finger; with your other hand lower the bag into a bucket of cold water – the water forces almost all the air out

and you then have an almost vacuum seal. Twist the neck of the bag tightly and fasten with a plastic- or paper-covered wire tie. Dry, label, and freeze. All packs should be labelled giving the following information: type of food, date frozen and any further information about its future use. Remember it may not be you who takes the pack out, so give as much information as you think necessary. Only by doing this can you hope to have and maintain good freezer management, for it is impossible to remember details of everything you put in the freezer. By the way, if you choose to use the adhesive type label, these do have a special adhesive to withstand the sub-zero temperature. It is so much easier to stick the label on the flat surface of the bag before putting the food in. It can also be very helpful to use different coloured labels for different groups of food, e.g. red for meat, green for vegetables, blue for fruit. The information should be written on the label using either a chinagraph pencil or a special freezer felt pen. Ordinary ink is not suitable as it tends to become smudged.

Alcan Polyfoil, packaging experts in the freezer market, produce a wide range of freezer products which are available from supermarkets, household stationery departments, multiple chemists and freezer centres all over the country. Among these is Alcan foil – which can be used for cooking, wrapping or freezing food. Alcan see-through freezer wrap, a self-sealing plastic film, protects food safely in the freezer over long periods without the need for freezer tape. Their freezer bags in three sizes enable you to freeze and store food in exactly the amount required. Invaluable also are the foil dishes, plates and freezer trays. (See illustration above for the full range). In addition the Alcan Freezer Advisory Service, 38 Berkeley Square, London W1X 6BS, will answer queries on freezer packaging etc.

JUST A FEW THINGS TO REMEMBER BEFORE STEPPING INTO THE WORLD OF FOOD FREEZING

Your freezer and your refrigerator

Your freezer operates at temperatures of zero and below. This is much colder than your refrigerator, which operates at temperatures above freezing, normally 6 degrees above. This means, therefore, that your freezer serves an entirely different purpose. It is designed for the preservation and storage of foods over long periods. You can't do without your refrigerator when you become a freezer owner – you will still need if for keeping the milk, butter, salad plants, etc.

Plan ahead

Make a list of the foods you would like to freeze. Think about your family needs, such as their ages, likes and dislikes. It's pretty pointless using up valuable space storing food which you know that they really don't like. Think too about the number of times you are likely to serve any kind or variety of food. You know the size of your family's appetite, so pack in quantities which you will need for one meal.

Foods to freeze

Careful selection of the foods you freeze has a great deal to do with their quality when eaten. Select foods of top quality – ripe, and free of blemishes – and freeze them at the time, if possible, when they would be best eaten fresh. Fruits and vegetables picked early in the morning are best, but this I know will not always be possible. Remember freezing does not improve the quality of anything, it merely arrests spoilage and maintains whatever quality the food has at the start.

Do not overload the freezer

Read carefully the operating instructions supplied with your freezer, and freeze only the quantity of fresh food in any twenty-four hours as recommended by the manufacturer. The fast freeze control should be switched on approximately six hours before a load of fresh food is frozen. This lowers the temperature inside the cabinet and allows the fresh food to freeze quickly.

Freeze only fresh food

Prepare fruits and vegetables for freezing just as soon after they are picked as possible – get all the family to help for the quicker you get them into your freezer the better. This is important not only because the frozen food will have a finer colour, flavour and texture, but vitamins are lost every hour that passes between the garden and the freezer, so only harvest quantities which can be frozen in twenty-four hours. The speed at which you work rewards you handsomely in the increased goodness of the foods on your table.

Don't keep frozen foods too long

Date all foods at the time of freezing and always use first those that have been stored longest. Try to use one season's crop before the next one is ready. To begin with this is quite difficult, as you have never before had to estimate just how much your family will eat in twelve months, but there is nothing more infuriating than having last year's cauliflower in the freezer when this year's is ready for harvesting.

The maximum time you should keep food in your freezer is twelve months. Most frozen foods will keep for that length of time, but I would suggest that you use certain food such as fatty fish, game, pork, baking, and other prepared foods within less time. Much depends upon the condition of the food when frozen. Quality produce and rapid handling in the preparation and freezing are very important factors.

2. The bulk buying of meat

Before you became a freezer owner the foods on which you spent most money each week were quite probably beef, lamb, and pork, and one of the outstanding advantages of being a freezer owner is having a good supply of various types on hand at all times, ready for immediate cooking and serving. Now that you are a freezer owner the money spent on meat will once again far exceed all other items which you will buy. It is important, therefore, to make quite sure that you really do *buy wisely*. The bulk buying of meat is a fairly complex subject and it is essential, therefore, to have a *reliable supplier*. A good butcher is master of an ancient craft. Like most skilled men he takes a proper pride in his work, and likes to be appreciated. His skills are at the customer's disposal. If you have a Dewhurst shop in your area, go in and chat to the butcher about bulk buying for your freezer. In Scotland, they trade under the name Munro. Dewhurst are, as you know, Britain's largest group of personal service butchers, famous for top-quality meat, and they offer to the housewife expert advice on the preparation of beef, lamb and pork for the freezer. They combine the old-fashioned craft of butchery with up-to-date shopping facilities and very competitive prices.

I am most grateful to Dewhurst for all the help which they have given me with this chapter, and I hope that the diagrams of carcasses and cuts (see pages 25, 27 and 28) will be helpful to you in your bulk buying. I have given the Scottish cuts together with the English cuts, as many of those sold in England would not be recognized by the Scottish housewife, and vice versa. I hope too that you will find the key on suggested methods of cooking helpful. From the hundreds of enquiries which I have had on this subject, I felt that it would be helpful at this stage to give a guide as to the cuts and weights you can expect when making a bulk purchase of meat. There are few housewives who know which cuts of meat come from which part of the animal and, apart from the financial outlay, you don't want to load your freezer with cuts which your family won't eat. Do make quite certain that you have enough space in your freezer to accommodate the bulk. Base your calculations on the following:

In every cubic foot of freezer space you can store on average 20–25 lbs. (10–12½ kg) weight of food, e.g. a 10 cu. ft. (283 l.) freezer = 200–250 lbs. (100–125 kg), 14 cu. ft. (396 l.) freezer = 280–350 lbs. (140–175 kg).

IF YOU ARE BUYING MEAT IN BULK IN ENGLAND

1. **SIDE OF BEEF:** Total Gross Weight Approximately 220–260 Pounds (110–130 kg)

   This is all of the forequarter and hindquarter. This really is an economy buy. Too large in most cases for one family, but ideal for two to share, offering you the widest variety of cuts at the best possible price.

BEEF

neck (EC)
mince (SC)
[C & S]

chuck (EC)
shoulder (SC)
[S, C & BR]

middle rib (EC)
shoulder (SC)
[PR]

fillet
[G, F & R]

topside
[BR, PR & R]

fore rib (EC)
standing
rib (SC)
[R]

rump (EC)
popseye (SC)

sirloin
[R & G]

[G & F]

[PR &
BR]

[S & B]

thin flank (EC)
mince or nine
hole (SC)

top rump (EC)
rump steak (SC)

shin (EC)
hough (SC)
[S & B]

brisket
[PR & B]

leg (EC)
hough (SC)
[S & B]

flank (EC)
boiling beef (SC)
[PR & B]

silverside
[B, BR & PR]

KEY	SC – Scottish Cut	R – Roast	G – Grill
	EC – English Cut	S – Stew	F – Fry
	BR – Braise	C – Casserole	
	PR – Pot Roast	B – Boil	

2. **FOREQUARTER:** Total Gross Weight Approximately 120–150 Pounds (60–75 kg)

Contents Roasting joints   Pot roasting joints
            Stewing steak   Braising steak
            Mince meat   Fat and bones – prepared for easy rendering, soup making, or for the dog.

3. **HINDQUARTER:** Total Gross Weight Approximately 120–150 Pounds (60–75 kg)

Contents Topside   Sirloin   Thin flank
            Top rump   Fillet   Leg of beef
            Silverside   Rump   Fat and bones

4. **TOPBIT AND RUMP:** Total Gross Weight Approximately 50–65 Pounds (25–32 kg)

Contents Topside   ⎫   Rump steak
            Top rump   ⎬ joints   Fillet steak
            Silverside ⎭   Beef skirt
                                      Leg of beef
                                      Fat and bones

IF YOU ARE BUYING MEAT IN BULK IN SCOTLAND

1. **SIDE OF BEEF:** Total Gross Weight Approximately 220–260 Pounds (110–130 kg)

2. **FOREQUARTER:** Total Gross Weight Approximately 100–120 Pounds (50–60 kg)

Contents Pot roasts   Shoulder steak
            Brisket   Steak mince
                          Fat and bones prepared for easy rendering, soup making, or bones for the dog.

3. **HINDQUARTER:** Total Gross Weight Approximately 120–160 Pounds (60–80 kg)

Contents Rump steak   Silverside
            Topside roasts   Steak mince
            Fillet steak   Boiling beef
            Popeseye steak   Sirloin steak
            Slicing sausage
            Fat and bones

4. **RUMP OF BEEF:** Total Gross Weight Approximately 50–70 Pounds (25–35 kg)

Contents Silverside
            Rump steak
            Steak mince

5. **RUMP OF BEEF WITH POPESEYE:** Total Gross Weight Approximately 70–100 Pounds (35–50 kg)

   Contents   Fillet steak   Silverside
                    Popeseye steak   Rump steak
                    Steak mince

LAMB – WHOLE: Total Gross Weight 40–50 Pounds (20–25 kg)
All cuts as detailed in lamb diagram. English and Scottish cuts listed.

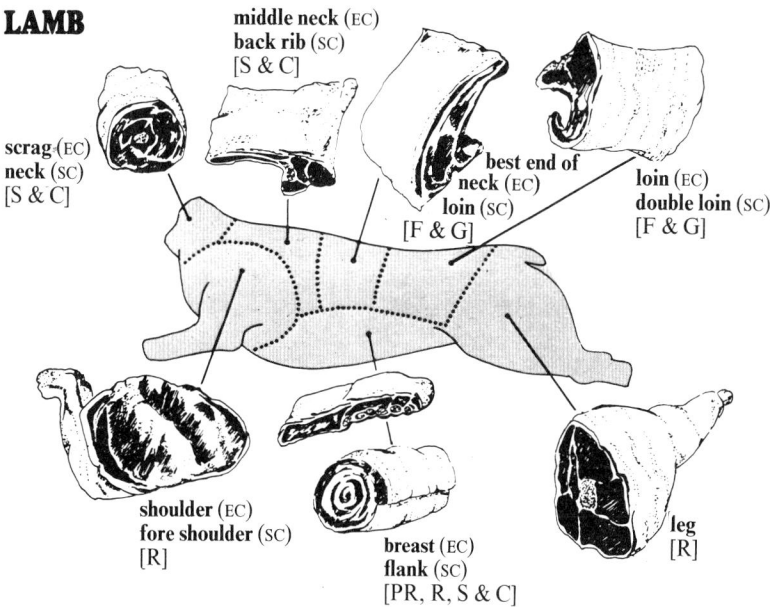

LAMB

middle neck (EC)
back rib (SC)
[S & C]

scrag (EC)
neck (SC)
[S & C]

best end of neck (EC)
loin (SC)
[F & G]

loin (EC)
double loin (SC)
[F & G]

shoulder (EC)
fore shoulder (SC)
[R]

breast (EC)
flank (SC)
[PR, R, S & C]

leg
[R]

SIDE OF LAMB: Total Gross Weight 15–20 Pounds (7½–10 kg)

English cuts Contents: 1 leg   Cutlets (best end neck chops)
                        1 shoulder   Chump and loin chops
                        1 breast
                        Stewing lamb
Scottish cuts Contents: 1 leg
                        1 fore shoulder Loin chops
                        1 flank   Double loin chops
                        Stewing lamb   Gigot chops

PORK – WHOLE PIG: Total Gross Weight 90–120 Pounds (45–60 kg)
All cuts as detailed in pork diagram on page 28.
English and Scottish cuts listed.

PORK

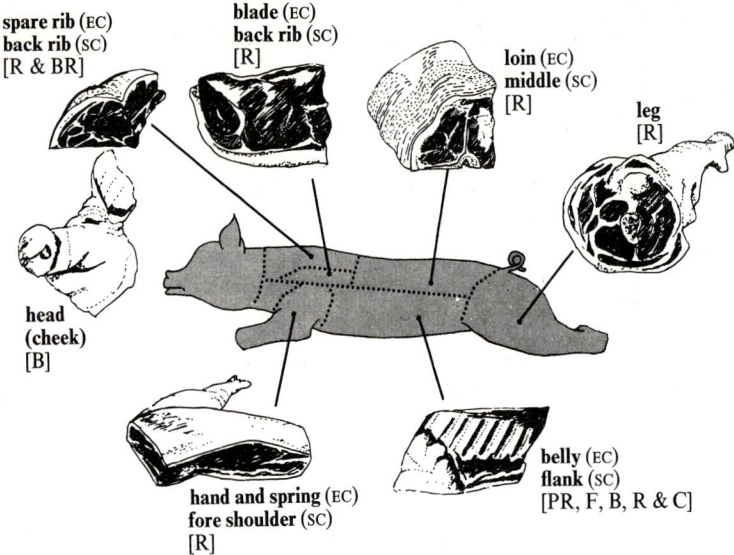

spare rib (EC)
back rib (SC)
[R & BR]

blade (EC)
back rib (SC)
[R]

loin (EC)
middle (SC)
[R]

leg
[R]

head
(cheek)
[B]

hand and spring (EC)
fore shoulder (SC)
[R]

belly (EC)
flank (SC)
[PR, F, B, R & C]

SIDE OF PORK: Total gross Weight 45–60 Pounds (22–30 kg)

English cuts	Contents:	Leg joints	Streaky joints
		Portion of head	Chops
		Spare rib joints	
		Blade bone joints	
		Loin joints	
		Hand joints	
Scottish cuts	Contents:	Leg joints	Flank
		(Gigot and Gammon)	Chops
		Buck rib joints	
		Middle joints	
		Fore shoulder joints	

When buying in bulk please remember that the price quoted per pound is what is called gross or dead weight – by the time it is butchered and all unusuable bone and fat removed the weight loss is quite considerable – between twenty-five and thirty per cent – but in my estimation it is definitely the best and most economical way to buy if you can afford the rather large financial outlay at the one time. I would strongly recommend that when buying in bulk you follow these three rules:

1. **Have your butcher prepare the carcase to your personal requirements**
   a. Joints – weights suitable for your family needs, state clearly if you wish to have joints on the bone, or boned and rolled.

b. Steaks -- packed in twos, fours and sixes. Thickness and weights to suit family requirements.

c. Steak for stewing, caserolling or braising in thick slices, or cubed for puddings and pies with kidney added, if liked. Mince in pounds or two pounds.

d. Bones for stock.

e. Fat or suet for rendering. (See page 48 for rendering instructions.)

2. Wrap and label *clearly*. Check that wrapping material used is recommended for long-term storage in the freezer.

3. Blast freeze if possible.

If these packs are not really suitable for your needs, then once again talk to your butcher. I would also suggest that you have a careful look in your local frozen food shop – they usually have a tremendous selection of meats to choose from. They offer steaks and chops in packs of five (2½ kg) or ten (5 kg) and mince in 5 lb. (2½ kg) packs, each pound (½ kg) individually wrapped, or you can choose joints of beef, lamb or pork.

On the other hand you may wish to freeze a bulk supply of meat yourself. If your favourite butcher will butcher to your requirements but won't wrap and pack for the freezer, and you feel that his quality and price are right and you have been buying from him for years, then follow these few simple rules:

1. Beef joints

Have joints boned if possible, they take up less space. If freezing with bones in, protect sharp edges and bones with freezer foil. Pack in polythene bag or wrap in freezer foil. Seal and label.

2. Steaks

Wrap individually in freezer film or place a double thickness of waxed paper between each steak and put in polythene bags – if you want to economize, the waxed paper from the breakfast cereal package is ideal; wrap tightly in polythene, seal and label.

3. Stewing or braising steak

Pack in polythene bags in weights suitable for your family needs. Seal and label.

4. Mince

Pack in polythene bags in weights suitable for your family needs. Seal and label.

5. Offal (Heart, kidney, liver, sweetbreads and tongue)

Soak in cold water for about 30 minutes. Clean well, drain and dry carefully. Remove any excess fat, valves and other tissue. Pack in quantities suitable for your family needs. Seal and label.

The same rules apply to lamb and pork.

There is, however, one big drawback to freezing down your own bulk supply – you will find that it will take you several days to freeze down a big bulk buy. Consult your freezer manufacturers' instructions as to the recommended daily freezing load.

I would *strongly* advise you to take only from your butcher the maximum recommended load each day, and leave the remainder in his cold room if he is agreeable. Perhaps you feel I am being over cautious, but when a big load of fresh meat is put into the freezer the freezing rate is very slow, and can cause toughening when you come to the cooking. Please don't blame the butcher. Serious overloading can activate the warning light – you will then probably 'phone for the service engineer, feeling that your freezer has developed a fault, and if the cause of this is due to overloading, you may find that you have to pay for this call. So please take my advice and follow carefully the manufacturers' recommendations.

MAXIMUM STORAGE TIME

Beef	– 12 months
Lamb	– 10 months
Pork	– 9 months
Mince	– 2–3 months
Offal and tripe	– 2–3 months
Sausages	– 6–8 weeks

Cured meats

Cured meats such as hams and bacons may be frozen. It is, however, important that they are very well wrapped, so that they do not dry out, or the smoked odour does not spread throughout the freezer.
The maximum storage time is very much less than for other meats.

Bacon joints unsmoked	– 6 weeks
Bacon joints smoked	– 10 weeks
Bacon rashers unsmoked	– 3–4 weeks
Bacon rashers smoked	– 4–6 weeks

Cooking of frozen meat

To thaw or not to thaw – that is the question which is always being asked. There does seem to be a wide diversity of opinion, so much so that the housewife who is fairly new to freezing and cooking from her freezer can really become confused. All small joints of meat EXCEPT PORK can be cooked straight from the freezer; I have found that the slow method of roasting gives best results, and although it is not absolutely essential I do advise the use of a roasting bag or roasting film, which not only saves time but means that you don't have to be continually basting during cooking – and it does help to keep the over clean. To use the slow method of roasting preheat the oven to 300–350 deg. F Gas mark 2–4, and remember to increase the cooking time $1\frac{1}{2}$–2 times. If you do have a meat thermometer use this to tell when the centre is cooked, but to avoid damaging the thermometer do not insert it into the joint until three-quarters way through the estimated cooking time.

For large joints, however, cooking from the frozen state requires a considerable amount of skill, if the meat is not to be served cooked on the outside while still almost raw and cold in the inside. For this reason many housewives prefer to thaw out large joints completely prior to cooking, but when thawing a large joint of meat you will notice a considerable quantity of the meat juice has been lost. Don't discard this – add it to the gravy. Large joints are best thawed out in the refrigerator, but this takes time – at least six hours per pound ($\frac{1}{2}$ kg). I would, therefore, advise you to take the joint from the freezer at least twenty-four hours before you want to cook it.

Chops, steaks, sausages and slices of liver can be cooked from frozen whether you wish to grill or fry, but until they are thawed out use only a gentle heat, and keep turning them to avoid any loss of meat juices. When thawed cook for your usual time.

Mince and stewing steak, or steak and kidney which has been cut up before freezing, can also be cooked from frozen, using again gentle heat until completely thawed.

PORK All joints and cuts of pork should be thawed slowly in the refrigerator before cooking.

As I have already said, one of the outstanding advantages of being a freezer owner is having a good supply of various types of meat on hand at all times, ready for cooking and serving. Here are a few suggestions for using the various cuts of beef, lamb and pork, which, if you have been buying in bulk, you will have in your freezer.

RUMP STEAK *Rump stuffed roast.* A large flattened rump steak is stuffed with minced chicken liver, ham, flavoured with herbs and onions and bound with egg. The meat is stuffed, rolled and tied and then roasted in a slow oven.

FILLET Bœuf en croûte is a fillet of beef weighing about 2 lbs. (1 kg) cooked in pastry. This makes one of the most impressive and easily cooked party or Sunday lunch dishes. In a very hot oven, cook the fillet for only ten minutes to seal the surfaces and keep the juices in. Make a filling with sautéed mushrooms, coarsely chopped – make a deep slit down the middle of the fillet and stuff with mushrooms. Season well. Allow the meat to cool. Place it on about one pound of rolled out puff pastry. Cover the meat with the pastry and see that it is completely sealed. Brush the pastry with some beaten egg and cook in a hot oven for about half an hour.

BRISKET *Pot au feu boiled beef.* Instead of using only carrots to make the traditional 'boiled beef and carrots', try using a variety of root vegetables. Poach rather than boil. A joint of 3 lbs. (1$\frac{1}{2}$ kg) will require about 2 hours cooking.

MINCE *Meat balls in mustard sauce.* Mix 1 lb. (½ kg) of lean minced beef with two slices of moistened bread to bind it. Fry the meat balls in deep fat. Serve them with a mustard sauce made from a thick white sauce flavoured with onions and mustard.

MINCED BEEF AND PORK *Moussaka.* Minced beef and pork are mixed and gently fried between layers of sautéed aubergines (to be authentic) and potatoes. The dish is topped with a rich béchamel sauce, and cooked in the oven until brown.

Keftedes. Add 3 lbs. (1½ kg) of finely chopped grated raw potato to 3 lbs. (1½ kg) of equal quantities of twice-minced pork and beef. Add a grated onion, season and add six well-beaten eggs. Make the mixture into walnut-size balls and fry them for 5 minutes in smoking hot, deep fat. Keftedes are ideal for a buffet party.

RUMPSTEAK *Bœuf Strogonoff.* Thinly sliced rumpsteak cut into almost matchstick-sized pieces, fried in butter. This is then added to sautéed Spanish onions and mushrooms mixed with French mustard and soured cream.

LEG OF LAMB *Roast lamb with pineapple.* For this dish score the joint in a diamond pattern. Pour the juice of an 8 oz. (225 g) can of pineapples over the meat, and roast it in a moderate oven, allowing about 30 minutes per pound (½ kg) of meat. Heat the pieces of pineapple and serve with lamb.

SCRAG Lancashire hot pot is best cooked in a deep casserole. Trim the fat from the scrag and casserole it in layers, interleaved with sliced potatoes, onions and root vegetables.

BREAST OR NECK *Navarin of lamb.* Dice the meat and brown it in a little hot fat. Casseroled with garlic and seasoning in a thick tomato sauce and served with diced carrots and peas, this is a delicious dish.

SHOULDER OR LEG OF MUTTON *Boiled mutton.* A gently boiled shoulder or leg of mutton, cooked with carrots, onions and plenty of seasoning and served with diced carrots and peas, is a thoroughly satisfying dish.

PORK FILLET OR TENDERLOIN *Fillets in sour cream.* Brown slices of fillet in butter, and simmer them for 10 minutes before adding sour cream. Thicken the sauce with flour.

CHOPS Pork chops with red cabbage and chestnuts. Trim all the fat off the chops, and cook in hot fat. Serve them with a casserole of red cabbage and apples. Cook the inner leaves of a red cabbage in butter for 5 minutes in a covered pan. Place alternate layers of the cabbage, quarters of apple, half a pound of peeled chestnuts, and slices of onion in a deep casserole. Sprinkle the layers with spices and add a little wine. Cook it until it is tender.

BACON AND GAMMON   Thick streaky bacon.
A hotpot of bacon.   Boil butter beans beforehand and place them in layers with cut up pieces of bacon and celery in a casserole. Add stock or water and cook until the bacon is tender.

COLLAR BACON   *Baked collar with cider.*   Blanch the collar bacon and simmer it in a mixture of half cider and half water. When it is almost cooked, take the bacon from the liquid and cut off the rind. Score the fat in a diamond pattern and cover it with brown sugar or black treacle. Put the meat back in the oven and baste it with some of the cooking liquid until the surface has formed a good brown crust.

LIVER AND KIDNEY   *Liver and kidney kebab.*   Remove all membranes from the liver and kidney and cut them up into large cubes. Marinate them in a little oil, lemon juice and herbs for an hour, with sliced onions, quartered tomatoes and mushrooms (if they are large), and thread all the ingedients onto a skewer. Arrange a sage leaf between the pieces of liver and tomato. This produces an excellent flavour. Brush the kebabs with a little oil and cook under a hot grill, turning the kebabs from time to time. Serve very hot with rice and quartered lemons and sprinkle them with chopped parsley.

LAMB OR PORK LIVER   *Liver and onions.*   Remove all tough membranes from the liver and cut up the meat. Fry in a little hot fat with sliced onions, diced streaky bacon and thickly sliced apples. Add enough stock or water to half fill an ovenproof dish. Cover and cook in a moderate oven for about an hour.

3. How to freeze poultry and game

Poultry and game do freeze very well but the percentage of freezer owners who have the opportunity today of preparing and freezing their own is indeed very small. Most of us – particularly where poultry is concerned – buy already frozen from our frozen food shop, especially when we can take advantage of special offers. I always have at least a few roasting chickens and boiling fowls in my freezer – they are such good buys and so many satisfying and substantial family meals can be made from chicken. Use the carcases for stock, and chicken soup can be made in minutes with vegetables from the freezer. The macedoine or mixed vegetables already diced and frozen commercially are ideal, and with a few cubes of parsley added just at the last minute nothing could be easier. Another very good buy in frozen poultry is chicken portions. Buy a mixed bag of wings and breasts, legs and thighs.

Poultry should be prepared for freezing in the following manner:

CHICKEN, DUCK, GOOSE, TURKEY

The birds should be starved for twenty-four hours before killing, but should be given plenty of water to drink during that time. After killing they should be plucked immediately, and it makes the job easier if they are plucked while still warm. With ducks and geese plucking is easier if they are plunged into near boiling water for 2–3 minutes. After plucking the birds should be hung by the feet for at least twenty-four hours in a cool place. If a more mature flavour – which so many people find lacking in mass-produced birds – is required, heavier birds i.e. over 5 lbs. (2½ kg) can be hung for forty-eight hours. Birds should then be *clean drawn* and any surplus fat inside removed before trussing.

Overwrap sharp bone ends with freezer foil to prevent the bag being pierced during storage. Giblets should be packed in a separate bag, but not inside the carcase, and slipped into the bag with the bird. Extract as much air from the bag as possible before sealing and labelling.

If you wish to prepare the stuffing at the same time, this should be packed separately, and then the bird can be stuffed when completely thawed out.

GAME BIRDS – Pheasant, grouse, wild duck, wood pigeon, woodcock

These are delicacies enjoyed – and sometimes not always appreciated – by the families of the shooting fraternity. Shooting is a very expensive hobby these days: no longer can one really afford to give away the spoils of a good bag. All game birds should be hung by the neck in a cool place before plucking and trussing, for at least four days or until the degree of maturity is reached to suit personal taste. The birds are more easily plucked if plunged into boiling water for 2–3 minutes. They should then be prepared for freezing, as for poultry, but do not freeze the giblets of game birds. Smoked pheasant is a real treat and if your husband has had a good season you might be able to find someone who would do this for you. It really is an excellent product to freeze, and a winner for that important dinner party.

RABBIT AND HARE

These should be paunched and hung by the hind legs, rabbit for one day, hare for two days or longer, until the degree of maturity is reached to suit personal taste. They should then be skinned, cleaned and jointed ready for cooking. Care should be taken in the wrapping for freezing as there is very little fat on rabbit or hare. Careful wrapping is important to prevent dehydration.

The blood of the hare, slightly salted, can be frozen separately, as it is used in jugging. In Scotland it is also used in the making of hare soup. If time permits when preparing rabbit and hare, they can, of course, be cooked before freezing.

VENISON

Must be matured before skinning and jointing.

THAWING

All poultry and game MUST BE COMPLETELY thawed before cooking. Chicken, duck, goose and all game birds should be allowed to thaw in a refrigerator for twenty-four hours or twelve hours at room temperature.

TURKEY

2 days in a refrigerator
1 day at room temperature.

LARGE TURKEYS

3 days in a refrigerator
2 days at room temperature.

MAXIMUM STORAGE TIME

Fat hens, Turkeys, ducks	– 9 months
Chickens	– 12 months
Game birds, goose, venison	– 6–8 months

4. How to freeze fish and shellfish

You should really only consider the freezing of fish if your husband's hobby is fishing or if you live in or near a fishing port because, of all the foods suitable for freezing, fish deteriorates in quality more rapidly than any other. It must be frozen while it is still *very fresh* – in fact not more than twenty-four hours after being caught.

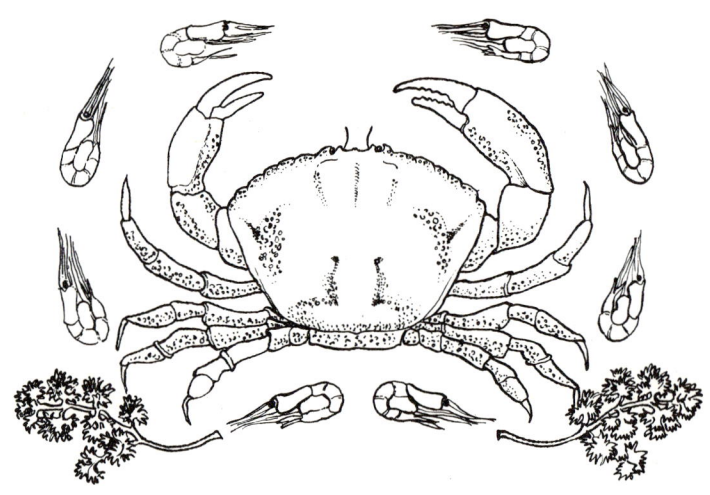

Prepare the fish as you would normally, i.e. gut, scale and trim fins; remove also the head and tail if you wish, but this is not necessary. Wash thoroughly. Small fish, e.g. whiting, brown trout, mackerel or herring may be frozen whole, but large fish should be cut into steaks or filleted. White fish fillets can be soaked in chilled salt water for twenty minutes before freezing – this firms the flesh and reduces the leakage when thawed. Pack fish in quantities suitable for one meal, and separate each fillet with a piece of greaseproof paper, or waxed paper saved from the breakfast cereal packet. There is also a special wrapping called Polytish which can be purchased from Lakeland Plastics, which is greaseproof and vapour-proof. Pack in polythene bags, remove as much air as possible, seal and label. If liked, white fish fillets can be prepared ready for frying in egg and breadcrumbs – these fillets should be frozen individually on trays, packed and sealed.

When preparing fish in quantity for freezing, care should be taken that no fish odour is transferred to the outside of the outer packaging. Remove the fishy smell from your hands by washing thoroughly in lukewarm water which contains several slices of lemon. Glazing with ice is another method of protecting the flavour of whole fish during storage. This is a.time-consuming job and I consider it only worthwhile for sea trout and small salmon. Fortunately, I have several keen salmon fishers in my family who always remember that I have a freezer and I enjoy sharing out of season game fish with my friends, or serving it on special family occasions.

To glaze, first freeze unwrapped and as soon as the fish is rigid submerge in cold water, just above freezing point. The zero temperature of the fish will cause a thin layer of ice to form – place the fish on a wire tray in the freezer. Repeat the process several times until the glaze is about one-sixteenth of an inch thick. Wrap well in polythene and seal. There are special polythene bags for salmon which are available from Coldstore Packaging.

THAWING FROZEN FISH
Large whole fish, salmon and sea trout should be allowed to thaw wrapped, in a refrigerator. If it is cooked before thoroughly thawed it will lack true flavour. Small whole fish should be cooked from frozen – but remember to allow a little extra cooking time.

STEAKS AND FILLET (*Either plain or dressed*)
Cook from frozen to your own recipe, but remember to allow a little extra cooking time.

SHELLFISH
Deteriorate even more quickly in quality than other fish, so it is of vital importance that they should be very fresh indeed, and once again it is really only practical to freeze them if you have a source of supply literally on your doorstep, or if your husband is a fisherman.

CRABS
Must be cooked before freezing. Place in boiling salted water using $\frac{1}{2}$ teaspoon salt to 2 pints (1 litre) of water, for 15–20 minutes. Cool quickly and thoroughly.

Remove the big claws and put aside. Lay the crab on its back with the tail towards you. With your thumbs push up the tail until the body comes away from the shell. Turn the crab around until the head is facing you, then remove and discard the small sac, containing the green matter and the lungs (dead men's fingers) from the top of the shell. If you are buying crab for freezing from the fishmonger, he will always be pleased to do this part of the preparation for you. Remove all the creamy brown meat from the shell. Split open the body of the crab and the big claws and remove the white meat.

Pack in polythene bags or containers, keeping the brown and white meat separate, if liked. Seal and label. Freeze immediately.

If you wish to use the shell at a later date for serving the crab, gently tap the inside edge of the shell, break it along the natural line to make a wider opening. The shell should then be washed, dried and oiled.

LOBSTERS

Must be cooked before freezing. Place live lobsters in boiling salted water for 20 minutes. Cool quickly and thoroughly. Split the lobster into two equal portions by inserting a large knife into the cross on the head, bringing the knife down through the tail, then, after turning the lobster round, bring the knife down through the head. Remove the sac from the head and the intestine, which is the thin cord running along the tail. Crack open the claws and remove the meat, together with the meat from the tail. Pack in polythene bags or containers. Seal, label, and freeze immediately.

The meat may be used in dishes prepared from cooked lobster, such as lobster Newburg.

Clean and store the shell if you wish to serve lobster mayonnaise.

SHRIMPS AND PRAWNS

These may be packed for freezing, shelled or unshelled, but packing unshelled reduces the preparation time when you serve them, and does save on freezer space.

Remove heads and wash in salted water and drain. Cook in boiling water for 6–8 minutes – cool quickly and thoroughly, shell if liked and rinse again under cold running water and drain. Pack in polythene bags, or, if you have a large quantity, freeze free-flowing then pack and seal.

MAXIMUM STORAGE TIME

White fish	– 12 months
Fatty fish, e.g. salmon, trout, herring, mackerel	– 9 months
Shellfish	– 1 month

Fish cakes are always popular either at lunch or supper time. They are easy and reasonably cheap to make, so if you have the time or if you really are anxious to economize, why not make some? They do freeze well and reheat very successfully.

BASIC RECIPE – 16 FISH CAKES

Ingredients:

1–1¼ lbs. (450–550 g) cooked white fish
  (you need 1¼–1½ lbs. (550–650g) raw fish)
 1 lb. (½ kg) mashed potato
  (you need 1¼ lbs. (550g) raw potato)

2 oz. (50g) butter or margarine
1 level teaspoon salt
Good shake of pepper
2 teaspoons lemon juice
⸴1 heaped tablespoon chopped parsley

For coating: Flour, beaten egg, brown crumbs or fish dressing.

Method: Remove skin and bone from fish if necessary, and flake coarsely. Add mashed potato, butter or margarine (melted if the other ingredients are cold), seasoning, lemon juice and parsley. Mix thoroughly and chill in the refrigerator until firm. Turn the mixture on to a lightly floured board, divide in half, and shape each half into a long roll. With a sharp floured knife cut each roll into eight pieces. Shape neatly. Brush each cake with beaten egg and coat with crumbs or fish dressing. Place fish cakes on a tray, lined with greaseproof paper, and freeze. When frozen pack in family sized portions, separating each one with a piece of waxed paper, or freezer film. Seal and label. Storage life – 2 months.

N.B. The fish cakes can be fried before freezing and then reheated in the oven, but I find that it is much better to fry in shallow fat or cooking oil, just before serving.

5. How to freeze vegetables

If you have a garden, pick vegetables when they are at their peak of growing perfection – early in the day if possible, when they are freshest. If you buy from a roadside stand or in the wholesale market, buy early in the season, so that you can be sure of getting fresh, firm produce. Select young tender vegetables just right for table use, freshly picked and in perfect condition.

PREPARE AS YOU WOULD FOR THE TABLE

Wash vegetables thoroughly in cold running water. Discard the imperfect and over-ripe ones for freezing, but don't throw these ones out – use them for a meal that day or the next. Sort or grade according to size if possible so that each package will be uniform.

BLANCH ALL VEGETABLES BEFORE FREEZING

Blanching, i.e. scalding, retards the action of the enzymes, the chemical agents which bring about undesirable changes in quality and flavour during the storage period. Blanching also makes vegetables easier to pack. The time for blanching varies with each vegetable and detailed instructions are given in the tables on pages 80–85. Blanch *only* one pound (½ kg) of vegetables at a time, using at least one gallon (4 litres) of water per pound (½ kg) of vegetables. If liked, you can add one level tablespoon of salt to each gallon (4 litres) of water. This helps to retain the bright

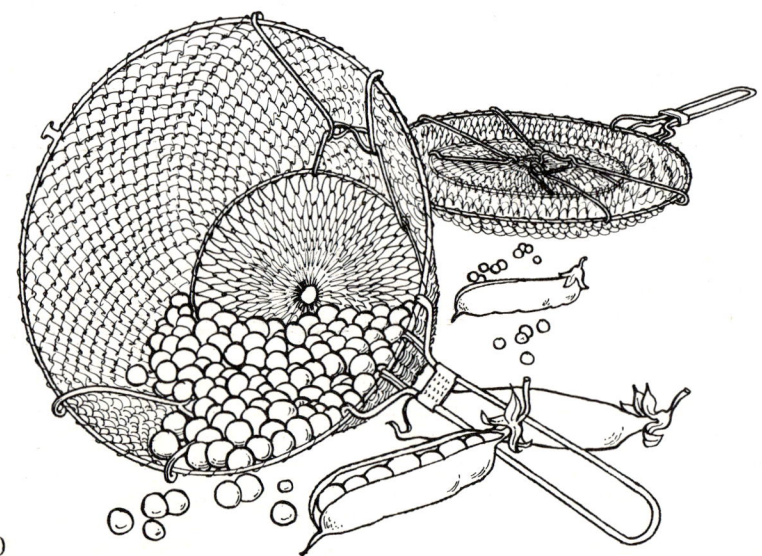

colour of freshly harvested vegetables. The same blanching water can be used six or seven times. For preparation of vegetables for the freezer you really do need to have the following pieces of equipment: one large saucepan which will hold comfortably 8 pints of water – your jelly pan will do, but if you are planning to freeze large quantities of vegetables you might like to keep a large pan for this specific purpose, as the surface will become very discoloured by the constant boiling; a blanching basket – there is now on the market a collapsible lightweight one which is ideal, and it stores easily when not in use. If you don't have a blanching basket and don't feel inclined to buy one, a fine white nylon shopping bag will do, or a roll of cheesecloth.

Pack in quantities suitable to your family's appetite. Seal and label – name of vegetable and date packed.

Free-flowing vegetables

If you wish to have free-flowing vegetables just like the ones you buy in your frozen food shop, after blanching, cooling and draining, spread out on swiss-roll or scone trays, lined with greaseproof paper or foil and freeze uncovered, but immediately they are frozen they need to be packed in polythene bags, sealed and labelled.

Place the prepared vegetables in the basket, nylon bag or cheesecloth and immerse in BOILING WATER. Begin to count the blanching time immediately the water returns to the boil. Please be accurate in your timing – use the timer on your cooker or a pinger timer. After blanching cool immediately either in a bowl of iced water or cold running water. A safe rule is to cool for the same length of time as the vegetables were blanched. Drain well – the vegetables don't have to be dried – use absorbent kitchen paper or a piece of terry towelling. Now they are ready for packing, sealing and labelling. Almost all vegetables can be packed for

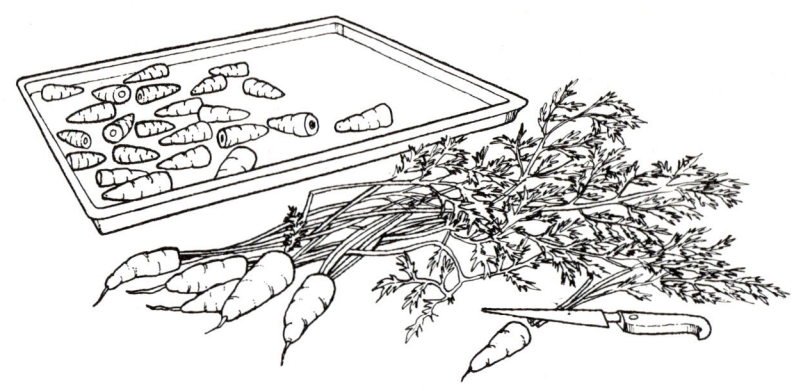

freezing in polythene bags – there are a few exceptions (see table of instructions for the freezing of vegetables pages 80-85).

Cooking home frozen vegetables

Remember, frozen vegetables have already been partially cooked in the blanching process, so take care not to overcook them before serving. All vegetables with the exception of corn-on-the-cob should be cooked from frozen – straight from the freezer into a pan of boiling salted water. Use only about $\frac{3}{4}$ pint (400 ml) of water to 1 lb. ($\frac{1}{2}$ kg) of vegetables. See instruction table for recommended cooking times.

There are many freezer owners who consider the blanching of vegetables a waste of time, but I would strongly recommend that you continue to do this, if your aim is to have really good vegetables of excellent quality. The main reason for blanching is to inactivate the enzymes, which, if uncontrolled, bring about deterioration in colour, texture, flavour and vitamin C content. Blanching also reduces the number of micro organisms present.

Much experimental work has been done in this field, and the only two vegetables which will store for a reasonable time unblanched, and retain fairly good eating qualities, are peas and small carrots.

6. How to freeze fruit

Choose firm, sun ripened freshly picked fruit in perfect condition. Over-ripe or bruised fruits should be frozen as purée. Most fruits will freeze well if the quality is good and you choose the correct method of freezing. For detailed instructions see tables pages 86-89. If you have a good supply of fruit in your garden, and if it is not possible to freeze the fruit immediately after picking, keep it cool in the refrigerator.

The short soft-fruit season can be hectic for the freezer owner – in fact it can be a daily chore.

BUYING FRUIT TO FREEZE

When there is a glut crop, fruit can be bought at reasonable prices from market gardens and local markets, or you can have a family outing to the local fruit farm, where you can pick your own. But remember – soft fruit bought cheaply at the end of the season will not be of the same quality as the more expensive fruit bought earlier in the peak of condition, but I do suggest that you take advantage of end-of-season bargains for pies and desserts during the long winter months when most fruit is very expensive.

METHODS OF FRUIT FREEZING

There are basically four main methods:

1. In dry sugar. Use about 4 oz. (100 g) caster sugar to each pound (½ kg) of fruit. Sprinkle the sugar over the fruit, making sure that it is well coated.

43

2. In syrup. Make a syrup using 6–12 oz. (175–350 g) of sugar to each pint of water (according to how sweet-toothed you are), and use about ½ pint (300 ml) of cold syrup to 1 lb. (½ kg) of prepared fruit. Remember to leave ½–1″ (1–2 cm) head space in each container to allow for liquid expansion, and place a piece of crumpled waxed or greaseproof paper

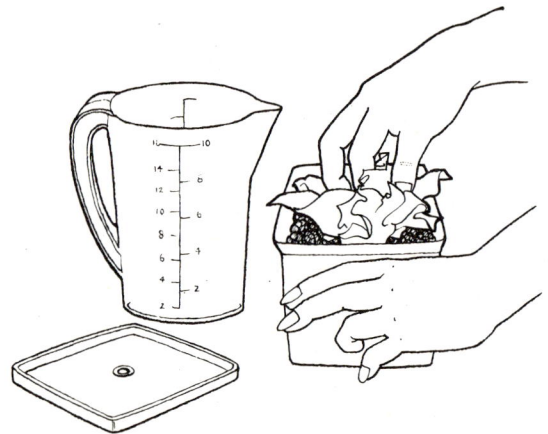

on top of the fruit before sealing down the container, to keep it under the syrup. This has to be done to prevent the fruit from becoming discoloured.

3. Free flowing. Spread prepared fruit on trays, without sugar – although sugar does improve the flavour of fruit you may be on a diet. For most fruits this is my favourite method of fruit freezing as I can then use it in whichever way I choose. Pack in freezer containers or boxes.

4. Fruit purées. Use fruits which are bruised, over-ripe or in any way not quite perfect. Put fruit into a pan and cook very gently over a low heat until the juice begins to flow. Rub through a sieve or place in a liquidizer. Sweeten to taste (I use icing sugar for this as it dissolves easily). Freeze purée in containers, glass jars or margarine cartons. Remember to leave head space for expansion.

Don't forget to seal and label
All fruit will keep in the freezer for 12 months.

Discolouration or browning of light-coloured tree fruits – particularly peaches, apples, pears, greengages and light-coloured plums – can be controlled by the addition of an anti-oxidant such as ascorbic acid. Ascorbic acid is sometimes available in crystalline form but you may have difficulty in buying it; it is however always readily available from your chemist in tablet form under its more familiar name of Vitamin C. Whether in crystalline or tablet form ascorbic acid should be dissolved first in a little cold water. Proprietary brands of ascorbic acid tablets state the number of milligrams present in each tablet, usually it is fifty or a hundred, and I would suggest that to each pint ($\frac{1}{2}$ litre) of syrup you use 1000 milligrams, i.e. twenty or ten tablets, dissolved in $\frac{1}{8}$ pint (75 ml) of water. This solution should be stirred into the cold syrup just before use.

An alternative to ascorbic acid is citric acid, available in crystalline form from your chemist. Dissolve $\frac{1}{4}$ teaspoon crystals in 2 pints (1 litre) of water. Allow the fruit to stand in this solution for *one* minute. DRAIN WELL before packing. Lemon juice is another alternative which can be used, but to be really effective it must be added in such large quantities that its flavour rather dominates that of the fruit, but if you wish to use it, add the juice of one lemon to 2 pints (1 litre) of water. Allow the fruit to stand in this solution for *one* minute. DRAIN WELL before packing.

FRUIT FOR JAM MAKING

The jam making season is a short one and a hot one. You normally find that you are making the jam and packing for the family holiday all at the one time. But with your freezer you can freeze the fruit and then make the jam when you have time.

BUT REMEMBER when freezing fruit for jam making a certain amount of the setting quality is lost. There is nothing more disappointing than runny jam, especially strawberry which is one of the more difficult fruits, so add at least ten per cent extra fruit to your own favourite recipe.

Fruit to be frozen for jam making should be packed dry in polythene bags, sealed and labelled, making sure that the weight of fruit is *clearly written* on the label. You might like to try making some uncooked jam which you must store in your freezer. It's so easy to do and the flavour and colour is quite superb.

STRAWBERRY JAM

Ingredients:
3 lbs. (1½ kg) strawberries   8 fl. oz. (200 ml) pectin
4 lbs. (2 kg) caster sugar

Method: Mash strawberries very lightly with a fork and stir in the sugar. Leave for about 30 minutes or until the sugar has dissolved. Add the liquid pectin and stir for 2–3 minutes.
Pack in small polythene containers (margarine tubs, waxed containers etc. will do), leaving about ½" (1 cm) head space to allow for expansion.

Cover and leave at room temperature for twenty-four hours until jellied. Seal and store in the freezer. Store for 6–9 months. Thaw for one hour before serving.

This jam should be used at one serving and, if necessary, stirred lightly to blend.

RASPBERRY JAM

Ingredients:

3½ lbs. (1¾ kg) raspberries 4 tablespoons lemon juice
4 lbs. (2 kg) caster sugar 8 fl. oz. (200 ml) liquid pectin

Method: Crush raspberries and put into a bowl with the sugar and lemon juice. Stir thoroughly and leave until all the sugar is dissolved. Add liquid pectin and stir for 2 minutes.

Pack in small polythene containers (margarine tubs, waxed containers etc. will do), leaving about ½″ (1 cm) head space to allow for expansion. Cover and leave at room temperature for twenty-four hours until jellied. Seal and store in the freezer. Store for 6–9 months. Thaw for one hour before serving.

The jam should be used at one serving and, if necessary, stirred lightly to blend.

N.B. Liquid pectin, e.g. CERTO, is readily available from chemists.

BANANAS

The freezing of bananas is not normally recommended as they are readily available through the year and they really don't freeze too well. However, if they are on offer at giveaway prices, they can be frozen unpeeled, individually wrapped in film or foil – the skin will darken but the fruit will remain a good colour.

As an alternative the banana can be sliced or mashed and packed in containers with lemon juice and sugar. I suggest you use soft brown sugar. They can then be used for sandwiches, filling for pastry cases, or as a dessert topping. A very good sandwich filling which is a great favourite with children, is mashed banana and coarsely grated chocolate.

7. How to freeze dairy produce

CREAM, BUTTER, FATS, CHEESE, EGGS AND MILK

All dairy products are readily available throughout the year, and as most have a fairly long storage life in the refrigerator it is hardly worth while storing these products in the freezer if space is limited; but bargain offers or visits to cash and carry warehouses are always tempting, and it is useful to have a small emergency stock.

CREAM

Double cream which is pasteurized and has a butter fat content of over forty per cent can be stored successfully. It is best stored whipped with sugar in cartons or freezer containers. If liked whipped cream may also be piped into large rosettes, frozen by the free-flowing method, and then packed in containers. The rosettes can be used to decorate cold sweets to serve with fruit or fruit pies. Cream thaws quickly, so it should be taken from the freezer just before serving.

N.B.   Cream, either double or single, which has been frozen commercially can be bought from your frozen food shop. This will keep very well in its frozen liquid state. The brand leader in this field must be Young's Seafoods, who market double cream in pints (600 ml), half pints (300 ml) and 3·2 fl. oz. (90 ml) jars, and single or coffee cream in pints.

BUTTER

If home made butter is to be frozen it must be made from cream which is not over mature in flavour, and should be *fresh* or only slightly salted. Commercially prepared butter should be over-wrapped with freezer foil or film before storing, in the freezer.

DRIPPING

Dripping home rendered from suet – normally included if asked for when purchasing meat in bulk – is well worth freezing, and should be packed·in waxed cartons or blocks – use any type of square cornered container lined with freezer foil to form mould. Remove from container when frozen, seal and if liked over-wrap in polythene.

TO MAKE HOME RENDERED DRIPPING

Cut beef suet or mutton fat, or a mixture of both, into small pieces and place in a strong unlined pan. Cover with water and heat gently until all the water is driven off. Carefully continue heating the fat until it becomes liquid and any solid remaining parts have become quite clear.

Then allow to cool slightly and pour through a fine-mesh metal strainer. Allow to become quite cold before packing. This dripping can be used for frying and making plain pastries and cakes

N.B. Careful watching and frequent stirring are necessary after the water is driven off.

MARGARINE
The storage life of this fat is long and it freezes well. The container or wrap in which it is packed is sufficient for freezer storage.

CHEESE
All varieties of cheese freeze well, and should be cut into pieces which will be eaten by your family within a few days after thawing. Allow one day in the refrigerator for defrosting, and another day at room tempera-ture for the full flavour to be enjoyed. Cheese for freezing should be wrapped tightly in foil and over-wrapped in polythene. The hard varieties of cheese are best grated and packed in jars or containers, ready to be used for cooking, and any odd piece of cheese which has gone beyond the attractive looking stage can also be grated and stored.

EGGS
Freeze eggs when they are plentiful and reasonably priced for use later when they are scarce and the prices are high. Eggs should never be frozen in the shell as this causes the shell to burst. Break eggs into a bowl and stir gently with a fork until mixed together. If the eggs are to be used for making buns, cakes, sweets or pudding, add about 1 teaspoon of sugar to every 2 eggs before freezing, and if to be used for savoury dishes, scram-bled eggs, omelettes, etc., add ½ teaspoon of salt to every 2 eggs. The eggs should be stored in usable quantities, clearly labelled salt or sugar.
When thawed, 2 tablespoons mixture equals 1 whole egg.
Egg yolks and whites may be frozen separately, but yolks have to be mixed with either sugar or salt to avoid thickness and gumminess when thawed. Yolks should be frozen, clearly labelled sugar or salt, in small containers – 2 oz. (50 g) Tupperware tumblers are excellent and can be used as moulds; when frozen the yolks can be packed in polythene bags. Ice cube trays may also be used.
One tablespoon thawed yolk equals 1 egg yolk.

EGG WHITES
The whites require nothing added and no mixing. They do not coagulate during freezing, and are packed in a similar method to yolks. They should be clearly labelled 'Number of whites'.
One tablespoon thawed whites equals 1 egg white.

MILK
Only homogenized milk freezes well, but this is not always available. Tuberculin tested and pasteurized milk will freeze, but will separate when

thawed. The appearance when thawed is rather off-putting and would not be suitable for drinking, but could be used in cooking.

If you live alone or if you would like to keep a few pints for emergencies, milk should be frozen in cartons. Milk bottles are not recommended for freezing. Milk with its very high water content takes a long time to thaw, and is best thawed at room temperature in the container. If needed in a hurry it can be heated gently.

MAXIMUM RECOMMENDED STORAGE TIME FOR DAIRY PRODUCE

Cream – 40% or more butter fat –	3–6 months
Cream rosettes	– 2 months
Butter, unsalted	– 4–6 months
Butter salted	– 2–4 months
Dripping – home rendered	– 6 months
Margarine	– 12 months

Cheese

Hard cheese	– 6–9 months
Soft and cottage cheese	– 4 months
Grated cheese	– 6 months

Eggs

Beaten whole ⎫ with salt or	
Beaten yolks ⎰ sugar	– 6 months
Whites	– 12 months

Milk

Homogenized	– 6 months
Pasteurized	– 3 months
Tuberculin tested	– 3 months

8. How to freeze macaroni, spaghetti, and other pasta foods

More and more families in Britain are becoming enthusiastic pasta eaters, and – contrary to many beliefs – pasta products such as macaroni, spaghetti, and all the others too numerous to mention, DO freeze well. Many exciting pasta dishes such as Lasagne and Cannelloni can be bought from your frozen food shop, just ready to warm through and serve. But, having bought your freezer for reasons of economy, pasta is still cheap to buy and there is absolutely no waste, so it is well worth preparing your own favourite dishes and freezing them.

Sauces to serve with pasta may also be made in quantity and frozen in family-size quantities.

TO FREEZE PLAIN PASTA

Use only good quality durum pasta and allow 2½–3 oz. (60–75 g) uncooked dried pasta per person. Cook in boiling salted water according to the directions given on the packet by the manufacturers, but for freezing REDUCE the cooking time by about 2 minutes. Rinse the pasta under cold running water immediately it is cooked, as this prevents it continuing to cook in its own heat. To prevent the pasta from sticking together, toss very gently in a little oil with a wooden fork. Pack into polythene bags or foil containers. Seal, label and freeze.

To use from the freezer

Tip while still frozen into at least 2 pints (1 litre) of boiling salted water, and allow the water to return to the boil. Drain and serve – this is sufficient time for the pasta to warm through.

SAUCES TO SERVE WITH PASTA WHICH FREEZE WELL

TOMATO SAUCE – for Spaghetti Al Sugo   Sufficient for 12 servings

Ingredients:

2 20 oz. (550 g) tins of Italian plum tomatoes or	Good pinch of mixed herbs
2 lbs. (1 kg) frozen tomatoes plus ½ pint (300 ml) of water	½ pint (300 ml) chicken stock
	½ teaspoon salt
2 onions, sliced	Freshly ground black pepper
4 tablespoons cooking oil	Tomato purée – amount added
2 cloves of garlic, crushed	depends on personal taste
	1 oz. (25 g) butter

Method: Fry the onions in the cooking oil for about 2 minutes and add crushed garlic. Add tomatoes, mixed herbs and stock. Season to taste.

Cover the pan with a well-fitting lid and cook to a pulp for about 20 minutes. Liquidize or rub the pulp through a hair or nylon sieve. Return to the pan and add tomato purée to strengthen the flavour. Use your own judgement as to the amount – this depends very much on personal taste. Add butter and gently boil until thick, stirring frequently. Allow to cool.

Pack the sauce in freezer containers in quantities suitable for family requirements. Seal, label and freeze. Storage life – 3–4 months.

When required remove from container and warm through gently from its frozen state.

Serve with cooked spaghetti which has been tossed in melted butter. Grated Parmesan cheese should be served separately.

Note This is a very traditional Italian sauce giving a true fresh tomato flavour.

BOLOGNESE SAUCE – for spaghetti Bolognese Sufficient for 12 servings

Ingredients:

6 rashers streaky bacon
4 oz. (100 g) butter
4 medium-sized onions, finely chopped
1 clove garlic, crushed
4 carrots, coarsely grated
4 stalks of celery, finely chopped
2 lbs. (1 kg) minced beef or, if available:

1 lb. (½ kg) minced beef
8 oz. (225 g) minced veal
8 oz. (225 g) minced pork
½ pint (300 ml) chicken stock
½ pint (300 ml) dry white wine

} or 1 pint (½ l.) chicken stock

1 20 oz. (550 g) tin of Italian plum tomatoes or:
1 lb. (½ kg) of frozen tomatoes plus ¼ pint (150 ml) of water
3 tablespoons tomato purée
1½ teaspoons salt
Freshly ground black pepper
1 clove
Pinch of grated nutmeg
12 oz. (350 g) sliced mushrooms

Extra additions if liked:

Ingredients:

6 chicken livers, chopped

8 tablespoons double cream

Method: Melt the butter in a frying pan, add the chopped bacon and fry for 2 minutes. Add chopped onions and garlic and cook for a further 2 minutes without browning. Add the carrots and celery and allow to cook gently for a few minutes longer. Remove vegetables and bacon from the frying pan and transfer to a large saucepan. Brown the minced beef and then add this to the vegetable mixture, together with the stock, wine, tomatoes, tomato purée, seasoning, spices, mushrooms and chicken livers (if used). Simmer gently, stirring occasionally, for approximately 1 hour.

Allow to cool. Pack the sauce in freezer containers in quantities suitable for family requirements.

Seal, label and freeze. Storage life in freezer – 3–4 months.

When required remove from container and warm through gently from its frozen state, and just before serving stir in if liked a little double cream – 2 scant tablespoons per four portions.

Serve with cooked spaghetti which has been tossed in melted butter. Grated Parmesan cheese should be served separately. A garnish of black olives is traditional but not necessary.

9. How to freeze home baking

Batch-baking when you have a freezer makes a lot of sense. It's just as easy to fill the oven with cakes and pies as switching on for one. It saves time – and what a saving there is too on the fuel bill.

Don't think that batch-baking increases your work load – it doesn't – you've got out all the equipment anyway, and you still have to do the washing up. It's the wise housewife who trebles her recipe for scones and fills the oven to capacity with other goodies. You may find that you have to invest in a few new tins – there's nothing more infuriating than finding that you are held up for lack of them. Cakes, buns, biscuits, fruit loaves and pastries all freeze particularly well. In fact, I know of many housewives who say that their baking actually improves with freezing.

Bread freezes very well and there is nothing more enjoyable than home made bread. So many families can find themselves in 'queer street' if, for some reason or other, commercially baked bread is not available – so why not make your own?

WHITE BREAD

Ingredients:

½ pint (300 ml) warm water
1 teaspoon honey or sugar
1 oz. (28 g) fresh yeast *or*
½ oz. (14 g) dried yeast
3 lbs. (1½ kg) bread flour

1 oz. (25 g) lard or 2 tablespoons oil
1 tablespoon salt
1 pint (½ l.) warm water or milk and water

Yield: 5 lb. (2½ kg) dough or 4 × 1 lb. (450 g) loaves
Oven: 450 deg. F Gas Mark 8
Baking Time: 40–45 minutes.

Method: Place the warm water, sugar or honey, and 1 teaspoon flour in a small basin. Crumble in the fresh yeast, or, if using dried yeast, sprinkle this over the surface of the water. Leave until the surface appears frothy – about 30 minutes.

Sieve together the flour and salt and either rub in the lard or stir in the oil. Combine together in a large bowl the frothy yeast mixture, the flour mixture, and the pint of water (or milk and water) and work to a soft firm dough which leaves the bowl clean. More water may be added at this stage if the mixture feels too dry. Knead the dough on an unfloured board, or in a mixer set at a low speed and fitted with a dough hook attachment, until the dough is firm and elastic. Place the dough inside an oiled polythene bag, secure the mouth of the bag, and put to rise (see note below) until it has doubled in size and springs back when pressed lightly with the fingers. Knead or 'knock back' the dough for a further 5 minutes by hand or with a mixer. At this stage it may be called 'risen white dough'. It is now ready for shaping into loaves. Divide the mixture into four pieces, each weighing about $1\frac{1}{4}$ lbs. ($\frac{1}{2}$ kg). Shape each piece and place in a greased and floured tin. Brush the top with oil and put to rise in a polythene bag until it has doubled in size.

Brush the surface with salty water for a crusty loaf. Bake in the centre of a hot oven for 40–45 minutes. To get some steam in the oven and improve the rise, pour $\frac{1}{2}$ pint (300 ml) boiling water into a meat tray and place in the oven. To test when the loaf is done, turn out onto an oven cloth and tap the base; it will sound hollow when the loaf is cooked.

N.B. **Rising or proving yeast mixtures** The time taken for a yeast dough to rise is as follows:

About 30 minutes in a warm place (for example an airing cupboard)

1 hour at room temperature (kitchen)
4 hours in a cool place (larder)
overnight in a domestic refrigerator

Where time permits, better results are obtained with yeast mixtures risen slowly.

SHAPING LOAVES AND ROLLS

If desired, the dough may be formed into loaves of various shapes or made into rolls.

Use the dough after it has been kneaded for the second time.

PLAIT $1–1\frac{1}{2}$ lbs. ($\frac{1}{2}–\frac{3}{4}$ kg) dough

Form three rolls about 14″ (35 cm) long. Pinch the ends together and plait loosely until half the roll has been used.

Turn over and continue plaiting to the end and pinch ends together to finish.

Place on a greased and floured tray, brush with oil, and prove inside a polythene bag.

Sprinkle with poppy seed if liked.

Bake as usual.

COTTAGE LOAF 1–1½ lbs. (½–¾ kg) dough

Divide the dough into two portions, one twice the size of the other.

Knead each and shape into a ball.

Place each ball of dough on a floured board, brush with oil and prove inside a polythene bag until risen to twice the original size.

Place the larger ball on a greased and floured baking tray and thoroughly dampen with salt water; place the smaller one on top. Make a hole through the centre of both rounds to the bottom and so fuse them together.

Notch the sides of both rounds with scissors.

Bake as usual.

ROLLS 1 lb. (½ kg) dough makes about 8–10 rolls

Dinner   Divide the dough into ten portions, knead each one, and form into a round ball against the hollowed palm of the hand.

Knots   Divide into eight portions, and form each into a roll about 10″ (25 cm) long; tie a knot.

Winkles   Form into 10″ (25 cm) long rolls as for knots. Wind each into a coil.

Brush the rolls with oil, rise to double the size on a greased and floured tray inside a polythene bag.

Bake at 450 deg. F, Gas Mark 8 for about 20–30 minutes.

To freeze: Thoroughly cool the rolls and loaves, and pack in aluminium foil or other freezer wrappings. Seal and freeze.

To serve: Either thaw in the freezer wrappings at room temperature for about 30 minutes for rolls, and up to 2 hours for loaves, or in a fairly hot oven, wrapped in foil, for 10–30 minutes.

SOFT BREAD ROLLS – Parbaked for breakfast

Ingredients:

½ pint (300 ml) water, slightly warm	2 lbs. (1 kg) bread flour
2 teaspoons sugar	4 teaspoons salt
2 oz. (56 g) fresh yeast, or 1 oz.	½ pint (300 ml) milk
(28 g) dried yeast	4 tablespoons cooking oil

Yield: 24 breakfast rolls

To parbake: 300 deg. F, Gas Mark 2, for 20 minutes.

To finish baking: 450 deg. F, Gas Mark 8, for 20 minutes.

Method: Dissolve the sugar in the warm water and crumble in the fresh yeast or sprinkle on the dried yeast; leave about 10 minutes until frothy. Sieve the salt and flour together in a large bowl and mix in the frothy yeast mixture, the milk, and the oil. Work to a firm dough which leaves the bowl clean. Knead for a further 5–10 minutes on an unfloured board. Rise in an oiled polythene bag until the volume is doubled. Knead again and divide into twenty-four pieces.

Roll each piece of dough into a round ball against the hollowed palm of the hand.

Place the rolls onto a greased and floured baking tray and place the tray inside a polythene bag. Put to rise for about 30 minutes in a warm place.

For parbaked rolls: Bake rolls in a preheated oven at 300 deg. F, Gas Mark 2 until set but not coloured, about 20 minutes.

To freeze: Cool thoroughly and pack in required quantities.

To serve: Return unthawed rolls to a floured baking tray. Bake at 450 deg. F, Gas Mark 8 for 20 minutes or until cooked.

For fully baked rolls: If desired the rolls may be completely baked at 450 deg. F, Gas Mark 8, for 30–40 minutes before freezing. They can then be cooled, packed, and frozen in the usual way.

To serve: These rolls may be thawed and reheated in foil wrapping in a fairly hot oven for about 10 minutes.

BROWN BREAD

Ingredients:

2 lbs. (1 kg) wholemeal flour
1 oz. (28 g) yeast or ½ oz. (14 g) dried yeast
2 oz. (50 g) lard

½ teaspoon sugar
1 pint (300 ml) lukewarm milk and water
2 teaspoons salt

Method: Make as for white bread.

Bread from the supermarket

The bread which you buy in the supermarket or from the baker freezes well if it is put into the freezer while it is still fresh. If you buy unsliced bread and you know that your family won't eat the whole loaf at the one time, it's a good idea to cut the loaf in half before freezing, then you will be able to take out just what you need. I always say that when you have a freezer you never waste food, not even a slice of bread. Store the bread in polythene bags. To thaw leave at room temperature for 3–6 hours. If you are storing sliced bread, individual slices thaw out in about 10–15 minutes. Sliced bread for toast can be taken straight from the freezer and popped into the toaster or under the grill.

CAKES, BUNS AND TEABREADS

Swiss rolls, fatless sponges and sandwich cakes, madeira type and lightly fruited mixtures, freeze perfectly. Rich fruit cakes and Christmas cakes can be frozen, but these keep well anyway so it really is a waste of valuable freezer space.

Sponge sandwich cakes can be filled and decorated with a butter cream or fudge type filling, or simply sandwiched together with jam or lemon curd, but if you wish to coat a sponge sandwich with water icing, this should be done after the cake has thawed and is ready for serving. Uniced cakes keep very well for up to six months in the freezer.

If you plan to freeze a number of sandwich cakes or fatless sponges a very good buy, to be sure of perfection in storage, is an 8" (20 cm) Tupperware cannister, in which you can freeze four or five 6", 7", or 7½" (15, 17, 19 cm) cakes with a round of greaseproof or waxed paper separating each one. Filled and decorated cakes should be frozen unwrapped and then stored in Tupperware.

Plain buns, scones and teabreads can be stored in polythene bags, but care should be taken, especially if you have a chest type freezer, that heavy packs of food are not stored on top of them. Set aside one of the baskets for these items or invest in an extra stacking basket. It can be disappointing to have these damaged due to bad packing arrangements.

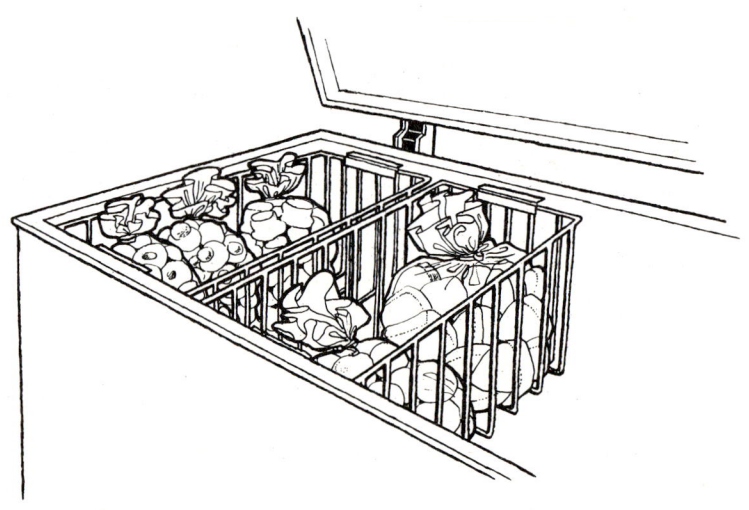

To thaw uniced cakes, take the number which you require from the container in which they have been frozen, place them on a cooling tray and cover with a tea towel. Decorated cakes may be left in the container in which they were stored, but remove seal while thawing.

APPROXIMATE THAWING TIMES

Small cakes	–	1 hour at room temperature
Sponge sandwiches or flan cases	–	1½–2 hours
Swiss rolls	–	2½ hours
Large plain cakes and gâteaux	–	4 hours

Cream sponges are best thawed in the refrigerator.

The luscious array of cakes and cookies above will give you some idea of what kinds of home baking to pack in the different shapes of Tupperware.

Lemon cheesecake pie (see recipe overleaf) is on the far right of the picture and above and below it are the orange sorbet (for recipe, see page 77), and raspberry mousse.

The recipe for orange topknots (*centre front, middle row in oblong box*) is also given overleaf.

Other items include chocolate-filled Swiss rolls and uniced cup cakes, custard flans, sponge cake layers, gâteau, pastry shells and small iced cakes. You'll have your own favourite recipes for these; if not, they're all in Good Housekeeping's cookbooks. (Photo courtesy of Good Housekeeping Institute).

Rigid Tupperware saves your 'light as air' cakes and buns from damage. There is never any problem when re-sealing a container after you have taken out the number of buns or cakes you need. There are sizes and shapes ideally suited for the storage of all your baking in the freezer.

ORANGE TOPKNOTS

Ingredients:

3 oz. (75 g) butter
3 oz. (75 g) caster sugar
1 large egg
1 level teaspoon grated orange rind

5 oz. (150 g) self-raising flour
1 tablespoon orange juice
Orange butter cream for filling
Little icing sugar

Method: Grease 12 2″ (5 cm) patty tins or place 12 paper cake cases into patty tins.

Cream butter and sugar; add egg, beating. Add orange rind to the flour and fold into the creamed mixture alternately with the juice. Half-fill the patty tins or paper cases and bake above the centre of the oven at 400 deg. F, Gas Mark 6, for 15–20 minutes.

Cool on a wire rack. When cold, cut a small circle from the top of each cake, pipe in a whirl or orange butter cream.

Replace the 'topknot'. Pack cakes in a single layer in a rigid container; seal and freeze.

To use: Dust with icing sugar after the cakes have thawed.

LEMON CHEESECAKE PIE

Ingredients:

6 oz. (175 g) digestive biscuits
3 oz. (75 g) caster sugar
3 oz. (75 g) butter, melted
1½ one-pint (600 ml) packets of
   lemon jelly
3 tablespoons water
2 eggs, separated

¼ pint (150 ml) milk
Grated rind of 2 lemons
4 tablespoons lemon juice
12 oz. (350 g) cottage cheese
½ oz. (14 g) caster sugar
¼ pint (150 ml) double cream,
   whipped

For decoration:

¼ pint (150 ml) (optional) double whipping cream

Method: Crush the digestive biscuits, place in a bowl and combine with the sugar and butter. Use to line 9″ 2-pint, (23 cm/600 ml) shallow open pie plate. Press into place with the back of a spoon. Chill.

In a small pan over a low heat dissolve jelly in the water. Don't boil. Beat together the egg yolks and milk, pour on the jelly, stirring, and return mixture to the saucepan. Heat for a few minutes without boiling. Remove from heat and add lemon rind and juice. Cool until beginning to set. Stir in the sieved cottage cheese, or blend the jelly mixture and unsieved cheese in an electric blender. Whisk egg white stiffly, add sugar and whisk again until stiff. Fold quickly into the cheese mixture, followed by the ¼ pint (150 ml) whipped cream. Spoon into the crumb crust, piling up slightly. Chill until set, then top with whipped cream before freezing (or freeze without cream and add the topping when serving).

To freeze: Place the pie in a Tupperware Pie Taker and seal. Store in freezer for up to 2 months.

To use: Leave to thaw, covered, at room temperature for 6–8 hours.

VICTORIA SPONGE

We all have our own favourite recipe for a basic Victoria sponge mixture – here's mine. I have used it for more years than sometimes I care to remember. The ingredient combination is very much different from any other Victoria sponge recipe, so please don't think that the printers have made a mistake.

Ingredients:

8 oz. (225 g) margarine	6 standard eggs
13 oz. (375 g) caster sugar	14 dessertspoons milk
1 lb. (½ kg) self-raising flour	1 teaspoon vanilla essence

Method: Cream margarine and sugar until light and fluffy. Add unbeaten egg gradually, beating well after each addition. Add milk and fold in the sieved flour with a metal spoon. Divide the mixture between four well greased 7″ (18 cm) sandwich tins, and bake in a moderately hot oven 400 deg. F or Gas Mark 6, for 25 minutes. Cool on a wire rack. When cold, fill and decorate if liked.
Place cakes in a rigid container.
Seal, label and freeze.

This basic recipe can be used in a variety of ways:

SLAB CAKE From which small fancy cakes may be prepared, iced and decorated.

QUEEN CAKES Add grated rind of a lemon, and currants.

RICH CHOCOLATE SANDWICH CAKE

Ingredients:

Reduce the flour by 1 oz. (25 g) add:	2 tablespoons brandy, brandy and
2 oz. (50 g) cocoa	water, or water
2 oz. (50 g) ground almonds	

Method: Sieve the cocoa and ground almonds together with the flour. Add the brandy when folding in the dry ingredients.

ORANGE SANDWICH CAKE

Ingredients:

Substitute 1 oz. (25 g) cornflour for	Grated rind of two oranges
1 oz. (25 g) flour	1 tablespoon orange juice

Method: Add the grated orange rind to the creamed margarine and sugar. Add the orange juice when folding in the flour.

PASTRY

All types of pastry freeze well but today many housewives take full advantage of the very good quality commercially prepared and frozen puff and shortcrust pastry, which is available in a variety of weights. It is always useful to have a few packs of each type in your freezer, but, whether you buy pastry or make your own, the habit of preparing several pies for storage in your freezer at the same time you are making them for immediate use is a good one to form. Having a pie ready to pop into the oven at a moment's notice, for either baking or heating, saves a lot of time, particularly on days when we are pushed beyond the limits of our endurance. When we have to cope with emergencies or the unexpected guests, fresh fruit pies which have been frozen are delicious.

UNBAKED PIES

Make pies for freezing in the same way as for baking, using foil plates or shallow foil containers. Before adding the filling brush the pastry base with egg white – this prevents the pie having a soggy bottom when cooked. Do not make slits on top until the pie is required for use. Place pies in the freezer uncovered until frozen and store in polythene bag, having first removed as much air as possible. Don't forget to label – you won't remember which type of filling you have inside each pie.

When required, cut the vents on the top and place the frozen pie in a pre-heated oven. Bake at the usual temperature, normally 425 deg. F, Gas Mark 7, allowing about 15–20 minutes extra baking time. As a general rule unbaked frozen pies have a crisper and flakier crust and a freshness of flavour superior to pies baked before freezing.

BAKED PIES

Bake pies before freezing if you feel that this method is more suited to your family needs. When pies are cold, wrap, label and freeze.

When required place the frozen pie in a moderately hot oven, 350 deg. F, Gas Mark 5, for 30–40 minutes, just long enough to defrost and warm through before serving. To serve cold, leave at room temperature 2–4 hours.

Maximum storage time – unbaked and baked pies – 6 months.

PASTRY SHELLS OR CASES

Either small individual or larger fluted flans are best fully baked before freezing, and should be stored in Tupperware – they are fairly fragile and you don't want to risk breakage.

The pastry recipe which I use for these was given to me many years ago by an old baker friend. It's foolproof and there is no need to bake the pastry cases with peas, beans or macaroni inside them to prevent them either rising in the middle or shrinking down the sides.

RICH SHORTCRUST PASTRY

Ingredients:

1 lb. plain flour ($\frac{1}{2}$ kg)
10 oz. (275 g) margarine
4 tablespoons caster sugar

4 dessertspoons cold water
Good pinch of salt

Method: Sift flour and salt into a bowl and add margarine cut into small pieces. Rub margarine into flour until mixture resembles fine bread crumbs. Make a well in the centre and add the sugar which has been dissolved in the water.

Mix well and knead until pastry is like a shortbread mixture. Roll out to an $\frac{1}{8}$" ($\frac{1}{4}$ cm) in thickness.

Choose a pastry cutter which is the same size as the top of the patty tins – this means that the pastry will come to exactly the top of the tin. Cut into circles and line the tins.

Prick well and bake in a moderately hot oven, 350 deg. F, or Gas Mark 5, for 12–15 minutes. Allow to cool.

Store as suggested in Tupperware.

The large fluted flans should be prepared, cooked and frozen in the same way.

The freezing of pastry shells or cases might be considered to be a waste of precious freezer space, but if you have a little space, use it. The pastry cases are a great standby, and can be served with a variety of fillings in the shortest possible time.

Here is an 'instant' filling which can be made almost as quickly as the kettle boils.

CHOCOLATE MOUSSE   Quantity sufficient for 8 pastry shells.

Ingredients:

3 oz (75 g) milk cooking chocolate
(I use Kake Brand)

1 egg
1 teaspoon top of the milk

Method: Place the cooking chocolate in a bowl over a hot, but not boiling, water, and allow to melt. Separate the white of egg from the yolk, and beat the white until stiff. Beat the yolk and the top of the milk together, and add to the melted chocolate. Fold in the egg white.
Fill pastry shells and allow to set.

This mixture will set in the refrigerator in about 5 minutes. Decorate with whipped cream. Use cream rosettes from your freezer, and chopped walnuts.

N.B. This filling is also most suitable to serve as a 'quick to make' cold sweet. Spoon the mixture over chopped pears, and decorate with whipped cream and toasted coconut.

VOL-AU-VENT CASES

Cut out ready for baking, are best stored uncooked. You can either make your own, if you are a really good puff pastry baker – I'm not, so I take advantage of buying in bulk from my local frozen food shop. There are many excellent well-known brand names to choose from. Jus-Rol offer a variety of sizes from cocktail to large entrée. These can be baked and served with a variety of savoury fillings.

One of the quickest fillings to make is scrambled egg and crispy bacon.

CHOUX PASTRY

This is one type of pastry which so many housewives seem to be afraid of making – I can't think why, because it has so many uses both savoury and sweet.

Ingredients:

2½ oz. (65 g) plain flour	¼ pint (150 ml) water
2 small eggs	Vanilla essence
1 oz. butter (25 g)	Pinch of salt

Method: Boil water and butter in a pan; sift flour onto paper and add to boiling liquid. Beat till smooth and cook very well. Allow to cool slightly. Add beaten eggs gradually. Beat well and then add vanilla essence.

Put the mixture into a large piping bag with a plain nozzle and pipe onto well greased trays.

For chocolate eclairs Use ½″ (1 cm) plain nozzle and pipe into 5″ (12 cm) lengths.

For savoury eclairs Use ¼″ (½ cm) plain nozzle and pipe into 2½″ (6 cm) lengths.

For profiteroles Use ½″ (1 cm) plain nozzle and pipe into small rounds about 1″ (2½ cm) in diameter.

To freeze: Freeze uncooked pastry on trays for 2–3 hours or until solid. Remove from trays and pack into suitable containers. Seal and label and return to the freezer.

To cook: Return the frozen piped pastry to greased trays and bake at 400 deg. F, Gas Mark 6 for 30–35 minutes. When well risen, brown and crisp, remove from the oven, make a slit along the side of each pastry and return to the oven at a lower heat, to allow the inside to dry out. Cool before filling. This pastry can, of course, be baked and then frozen either before or after filling, but if you choose this method, store in Tupperware or suitable containers for extra protection.

Thaw baked choux pastries at room temperature for about 1 hour, or if you need them quickly, in a fairly hot oven for 10 minutes.

Thaw filled cases in the refrigerator for at least 4 hours.

PANCAKES

Pancakes freeze well and it is useful to have these in the freezer ready to fill with sweet or savoury fillings. If you don't feel like making your own, these too can be bought, usually 12 to a box, in your local frozen food shop.

Use your own favourite recipe or try this one:

Ingredients:

4 oz. (100 g) plain flour
¼ teaspoon salt
1 egg plus 1 egg yolk (the extra white can be frozen for use at a later date)
½ pint (300 ml) milk
1 tablespoon cooking oil *or* melted butter

Method: Sift the flour and salt into a bowl, make a well in the centre, drop in the egg plus extra yolk, together with one third of the milk. Mix to a smooth paste. Beat well, gradually adding the remainder of the milk. Finally add the oil or melted butter.

Cover the bowl and allow the batter to stand for at least half an hour in the refrigerator.

Make the pancakes very thin in a hot greased pan.

Cool between a tea towel.

To freeze: Place a circle of waxed or greaseproof paper between each pancake. Pack, seal and label.

To thaw and make ready for serving: Place the number required on a baking sheet and cover with foil – warm through in a hot oven for 10–15 minutes.

Sweet fillings: Sprinkle with caster sugar and a little lemon juice – roll up and serve with whipped cream.

Spread with your favourite jam or marmalade – roll up and serve.

Fill with ice cream – roll up and brush with warmed jam.

Fill with ice cream and chopped nuts – roll up and coat with chocolate sauce.

Fill with fresh fruit and whipped cream – roll up and serve.

As an alternative to serving pancakes with a sweet filling, serve them with a tangy sweet sauce.

Savoury fillings: Fill with chopped ham in white sauce. Roll up and serve.

Fill with shellfish in white sauce. Roll up and serve.

Fill with diced cooked chicken and mushrooms, mixed with condensed mushroom or chicken soup. Roll up and serve.

10. How to freeze family meals

SOUPS   MAIN COURSES   PUDDINGS AND SWEETS

It would be impossible for me in this chapter to attempt to cover completely all the foods which can be prepared or pre-cooked before freezing, but I hope that by giving you basic information on bulk cooking for the freezer, and recipes which I know freeze well, you will build up a good reserve of family meals, either using your own recipes or trying some of mine, which you will find invaluable in the months ahead, e.g.:

1. In the event of illness.
   a. Your husband or your family may be ill and require your undivided attention, and there is just no time to cook.
   b. *You* may be ill – what a blessing a well stocked freezer can be in these circumstances.
2. Coping with unexpected guests.
3. Coping with school holidays.
4. Having friends visit for holidays – you don't want to spend too much time in the kitchen.
5. You want to have a few days off, away from cooking. Having prepared meals in the freezer is the answer.

HINTS ON THE PREPARATION AND FREEZING OF MEALS

1. Use ingredients which are fresh and of good quality. The ingredients which you use in the preparation of meals will, in most cases, be taken from the freezer, defrosted, cooked and re-frozen. For having been cooked they are then considered as being frozen for the first time. Therefore, meat can be re-frozen as stew and casseroles; chicken can be roasted or casseroled, and fruit defrosted and cooked in puddings and pies.

A good general rule to remember if you have any doubts about re-freezing of food is – Food can be re-frozen if you change its state from raw to cooked.

2. Cool foods as quickly as possible before freezing. I don't want you to think that I am being too fussy and giving you even more work to do, but the very best results are obtained by standing the food in its container in a bowl of cold water and ice cubes.

3. Remove excess fat from foods before freezing. When the food has cooled the excess fat will have formed fat globules and can easily be removed.

4. Fried foods must be thoroughly drained on absorbent kitchen

paper before freezing, and they must be quite cold before packing, in order to avoid soggy results.

5. Under-season all food to be frozen.

6. Slightly undercook foods which are to be frozen by up to 30 minutes, e.g. when preparing stews and casseroles; when preparing dishes using pasta it is most important to undercook, otherwise the pasta becomes very soft.

HINTS ON THAWING AND SERVING

1. Thaw soups, meat, fish and poultry dishes to be served cold in the refrigerator. The thawing rate is very slow, so take them from the freezer the day before you need them.

2. All dishes thawed at room temperature, or in the refrigerator, should be left in their freezer wrapping.

3. Casserole dishes containing meat, fish, poultry and vegetables can be placed in a cold oven, which can then be set at the temperature required.

4. For working wives who have cookers with automatic timers, frozen casserole dishes may be popped into the oven before leaving for work, and the controls set according to manufacturers' instructions. What a joy it is to come home, particularly after a very hard day, knowing that all you have to do is to lay the table and serve the meal.

5. Soups and sauces to be served hot should be thawed and re-heated in a saucepan, beginning with a low heat and stirring all the time. Where the soup or sauce is milk-based use a double boiler, if possible, or a bowl over hot water.

6. If soups and sauces appear to have separated, a good hand whisking during heating will restore the consistency.

7. Check on flavour and adjust seasoning before serving.

STOCK FOR SOUP

Meat, bone and chicken stock freezes well, and should be prepared in the normal way, ready to use as a base for fresh soup, or in stews, casseroles or sauces. Before freezing remove any fat from the surface. It can be stored in glass jars, allowing $\frac{1}{2}''$ (1 cm) head space, or line a rigid plastic container with a gusseted polythene bag – pour in stock and freeze till solid. Remove bag, seal and label.

A 1 lb. ($\frac{1}{2}$ kg) loaf tin can also be used for this, lined with heavy-duty foil. The frozen stock can then be stored easily, just like blocks or bricks. If freezer space is really limited, stock may be concentrated before freezing. After straining, boil the completed stock in a pan with the lid off, until the volume is reduced by half. Cool, pack and freeze.

SOUP

Soup is a very good example of a food which can be prepared in quantity with little extra work. It is just as easy to prepare twelve portions as four. Who does not welcome a bowl of hot soup on a cold day? Soup which is thickened with ordinary flour, tends to curdle on re-heating. Use cornflour to avoid curdling. Starchy foods such as rice, barley, sago, pasta and potato, become mushy when frozen in liquid, and I suggest that you add these to the soup during re-heating. Soups should be stored using the same containers as for stock.

During the summer lettuce is always plentiful and if we grow our own we always seem to have more than we can eat. Lettuce does not freeze well in its raw state, but it does freeze well as a soup.

LETTUCE SOUP   8–10 portions

Ingredients:

4 lettuce

2 oz. (50 g) dripping or lard

4 medium sized onions, roughly chopped

3 pints (1½ l.) meat or bone stock

1 pint (½ l.) milk

2 oz. (50 g) sago, oatmeal or semolina

Seasoning

Chopped mint

Method: Wash and shred lettuce. Sauté the onions in hot dripping for 5 minutes. Add the stock and bring to the boil. Add lettuce and seasoning, return to boiling point and simmer for 30 minutes. Blend in liquidizer or rub through a nylon sieve. Return to pan, add milk and heat to boiling point.

To freeze: Cool rapidly, remove any excess fat from the surface. Pack in suitable quantities for personal requirements.
Seal, label and freeze.

To serve: Reheat to boiling point and thicken with sago, oatmeal or semolina, and adjust seasoning. Just before serving add chopped mint.
Storage life – 3–4 months.

Cucumbers too are plentiful and cheap during the season, or you may have a glut crop of your own. Cucumber soup, served either hot or cold, is really delicious and most refreshing and, like lettuce, cucumber does not freeze well in its raw state.

CREAM OF CUCUMBER SOUP   Served hot – 8–10 portions

Ingredients:

3 lbs. (1½ kg) cucumber

2 oz. (50 g) butter

A good pinch of sugar

Paprika pepper ⎫ to
thinly sliced cucumber ⎭ garnish

Salt and pepper

½ pint (300 ml) chicken stock

½ pint (300 ml) single cream

For white sauce:

⅔ of a pint (350 ml) of milk

1 medium sized onion

2 bay leaves

1 oz. (25 g) butter

1 oz. (25 g) cornflour

Method: Make the white sauce by putting the milk, onion and bay leaves on to boil. Draw the pan off the heat and leave to infuse for 10 minutes. Melt the butter in a saucepan and stir in the cornflour. Gradually add the strained milk and bring back to the boil, stirring constantly. Cook gently for 2–3 minutes. Peel the cucumber and slice in half lengthwise – remove the seeds and slice thinly. Blanch in boiling water for 2 minutes then drain.

Melt the butter in a pan, add the cucumber, sugar, salt and pepper. Cover with lid and cook gently until soft.

Add the white sauce and chicken stock, cover, and cook for a further 15 minutes.

Blend in liquidizer or rub through a nylon sieve. Return to pan and heat to boiling point.

To freeze: Cool rapidly. Remove any excess fat from the surface. Pack in suitable quantities for personal requirements. Seal, label and freeze.

To serve: Reheat very slowly to boiling point. If you have a double boiler use it, if not reheat in a bowl over hot water. Stir in the cream. Garnish with thinly sliced cucumber and sprinkle with paprika pepper. Storage life – 3–4 months.

N.B.   This is an excellent soup to serve when entertaining. Your own supply of cucumber may be exhausted by the time you wish to serve this soup, but buying a small piece for garnish will not cost too much.

ICED CUCUMBER SOUP   8–10 portions

Ingredients:

4 lbs. (2 kg) cucumber	3 teaspoons tarragon
1 pint ($\frac{1}{2}$ l.) water	Salt and pepper
$\frac{1}{2}$ pint (300 ml) thick cream	

Paprika pepper   ⎱ to
thinly sliced cucumber ⎰ garnish

Method: Peel the cucumber and slice thickly. Boil with seasoning and tarragon for 20 minutes until tender. Blend in liquidizer or rub through a nylon sieve.

To freeze: Cool rapidly. Pack in suitable quantities for personal requirements.
Seal, label and freeze.

To serve: Thaw unopened in the refrigerator. Just before serving stir in the thick cream. Adjust the seasoning and garnish with thinly sliced cucumber and sprinkle with paprika pepper.
This is a most delicious starter to serve on a stuffy, sweltering summer day.

These soups are, of course, a bit out of the ordinary, but there is no reason why you should not make your own family favourites and freeze them. Just follow the basic freezing rules which I have given and all will be well.

MAIN COURSE CASSEROLES AND STEWS

Depending on your choice of meat and poultry, and the other ingredients which you choose to use in the preparation of stews and casseroles, you can create a nourishing family meal or a more sophisticated dish suitable for that special or important occasion. Stew and casserole dishes freeze well and can be re-heated on top of the cooker or in the oven within an hour, with little or no attention, and all you have to do before serving is to adjust the seasoning. Care should be taken when preparing main course dishes for freezing to make sure that there is plenty of liquid in these dishes to cover the meat or poultry completely, otherwise you may find that they will dry out.

Recipes may be specially prepared in large quantities, but personally I would suggest that you treble your family-size recipes – serve one and freeze two. By following this suggestion you can build up fairly quickly a good supply of main course dishes. Remember too that the recommended storage life of stews and casseroles is 3–4 months.

Remember to reduce the cooking time by up to 30 minutes on your own recipes, thus avoiding over-cooking during the reheating time. The cooking times given in the following recipes have been *reduced*.

BRAISED STEAK AND KIDNEY WITH SAVOURY PIN WHEEL PASTRY

Ingredients:
1½ lbs. (¾ kg) braising or stewing steak
½ lb. (225 g) ox kidney
1 tablespoon seasoned flour
½ pint (300 ml) of stock or use
2 cubes of concentrated stock made up to ½ pint (300 ml) with water
2 oz. (50 g) dripping

Pin Wheel Pastry

Ingredients:
8 oz. (225 g) plain flour
¼ teaspoon salt
2 oz. (50 g) margarine
2 oz. (50 g) cooking fat or lard
Cold water to mix
3 medium-sized onions, finely chopped
Beaten egg to glaze

Method: Cut steak into small cubes. Prepare kidney and cut into small pieces.
(You may have bags of steak and kidney in your freezer ideal for this recipe.)
Toss steak and kidney in seasoned flour. Heat the dripping in a pan until very hot, add steak and kidney and brown well. Gradually add the stock. Return to boiling point and simmer gently for 1½ hours.
Place the steak and kidney in a foil container of suitable size, or in a casserole which has been lined with heavy-duty foil. Allow to cool while preparing the pastry.

70

To make the pastry

Sift the plain flour and salt into a bowl, add the cut-up margarine and cooking fat and rub into the flour until the mixture resembles fine bread crumbs. Make a well in the centre, add cold water – about 4 fluid ounces (100 ml) – and mix to a stiff dough. Turn out onto a floured board and knead lightly till smooth. Roll out into an oblong shape until pastry is about ¼" (½ cm) thick. Turn pastry upside down and scatter over the very finely chopped onion. Roll up as for a Swiss roll – rolling from the longer side of the oblong. With a sharp knife – your freezer knife if you have one, is excellent for this – cut the pastry roll into 12 slices and arrange them cut side up on top of the steak and kidney. Brush with egg. Allow to become quite cold before sealing, labelling and freezing.

N.B. If using a casserole lined with heavy-duty foil, place in freezer and when frozen remove foil parcel and over-wrap in polythene. This means that your casserole is back in normal service again.

To serve: Remove cover from container, or return foil parcel to casserole which was used as the mould, folding back the foil to allow the pastry to cook.

Place while still frozen in a hot oven, 425 deg. F, Gas Mark 8, for 25 minutes until the pastry is cooked and golden brown. Lower the heat to 375 deg. F, Gas Mark 5, and continue to cook for a further 25–30 minutes.

If liked, serve with jacket potatoes which can be baked in the oven at the same time as the pie and a selection of vegetables from the freezer. Cauliflower au gratin may also be served.

This recipe makes 6–8 servings.

MINCED BEEF AND MACARONI PIE

Ingredients:

4 oz. (100 g) short cut macaroni
1 lb. (½ kg) cooked minced beef in gravy

2 tablespoons tomato ketchup
3 slices of white bread and butter

Method: Cook the macaroni in plenty of boiling salted water for 6–8 minutes. Drain and rinse under cold running water to separate the macaroni and to prevent it continuing to cook in its own heat. Drain thoroughly.

Mix the macaroni with the minced beef and tomato ketchup, adjust the seasoning. Place this mixture in a foil container or foil-lined casserole and top with sufficient buttered bread, cut into triangles, to cover. Arrange the bread buttered side up.

Seal, label and freeze.

To serve: Remove cover from container, or return foil parcel to casserole which was used as the mould, folding back the foil to allow the buttered bread to become crisp and brown during the re-heating time.

Place while still frozen in a moderately hot oven, 375 deg. F, Gas Mark 5, and bake for 30 minutes.

Lower the heat to 300 deg. F, Gas Mark 4, and continue cooking for a further 20 minutes or until the pie filling is piping hot. Serve with vegetables selected from the freezer, or with baked beans for the children. This really is a children's favourite.

Serves – 4–6.

This is an excellent dish to make if you have cooked several pounds of mince and, with the addition of the macaroni, it makes a pound of mince go a long way.

SAUSAGE AND CELERY AU GRATIN

Ingredients:

1 lb. (½ kg) pork sausages
   (8 to the pound if possible)

4 rashers of streaky bacon
1 large head of celery

Cheese sauce:

1½ oz. (40 g) butter or margarine
1½ oz. (40 g) plain flour
Salt and pepper and ¼ teaspoon dry
   mustard

½ pint (300 ml) milk
¼ pint (150 ml) celery water
3 oz. (75 g) grated cheese

Garnish:

2 oz. (50 g) button mushrooms,
   sautéed in butter

1 oz. (25 g) grated cheese

Method: Prick the sausages to prevent the skins from bursting and fry slowly for about 8–10 minutes depending on thickness, until lightly brown and half cooked. Drain on absorbent paper. Remove rind from bacon and stretch each rasher to double its length with the back of a round bladed knife.

Wrap half a rasher of bacon round each sausage and place in foil container or foil-lined casserole.

Wash celery and scrub if necessary, cut into 1″ lengths and cook in boiling salted water for 15–20 minutes. Drain and retain ¼ pint (150 ml) of this liquid.

Make up the cheese sauce. Cover the sausages with the celery and then pour over the sauce.

Garnish with the sautéed mushrooms and sprinkle with the grated cheese. Allow to become quite cold. Seal, label and freeze.

To serve: Remove cover from container or return foil parcel to the casserole dish which was used as the mould, folding back the foil to allow the cheese to brown.

Place while still frozen in a moderately hot oven, 350 deg. F, Gas Mark 5, for 35–40 minutes or until nicely browned. Garnish with parsley.

N.B. Leeks may be used as an alternative to celery, 1½ lbs. (¾ kg) of fresh leeks or 1 lb. (½ kg) of leeks from the freezer.

This is a most enjoyable supper dish served with hot crispy rolls and butter. It is a favourite of mine on winter Sunday evenings for a fireside supper.

CURRY SAUCE

Ingredients:

2 oz. (50 g) butter or margarine	2 peeled and chopped tomatoes
1 oz. (25 g) plain flour	1 lb. (½ kg) cooking apples
4 oz. (100 g) sliced onions	2 oz. (50 g) seedless raisins
1 oz. (25 g) curry powder	½ pint (300 ml) stock
4 oz. (100 g) sliced carrots	1 tablespoon Demerara sugar
1 oz. (25 g) tomato purée	Seasoning to taste

Method: Sauté the sliced onions in the butter or margarine to a deep golden colour. Add curry powder and cook well. Mix in the flour and cook the mixture again for 2 minutes. Remove from heat and gradually add the stock. Return to the heat and stir constantly until the mixture boils. Add all other ingredients and simmer gently for 40 minutes. Cool quickly. Spoon into two ½ pint (300 ml) containers. Seal, label and freeze.

To serve: Thaw slowly in the refrigerator or more rapidly in a double boiler, or in a bowl over hot water.

Serve with lamb, chicken or beef. Add the chopped cooked meats to the curry sauce when it has thawed and cook gently over boiling water for 30 minutes. Serve with plain boiled rice.

One of my favourite dishes is curried white fish. Few people seem to think about currying fish until it is suggested to them. Curried fish is a most nourishing main course dish, and there is always plenty of white fish available. You may even have a good supply in your freezer. Cod haddock and whiting are all suitable, and if it is available in your saithe or coley is excellent.

CURRIED WHITE FISH

Prepare the curried sauce as suggested.

Wash and dry the white fish fillets and cut into pieces about 1½"–2" (4–5 cm) in size. Place the raw fish in an ovenproof dish or casserole – season well with salt and pepper and pour over the juice of half a lemon. Spoon ¼ pint (150 ml) of curry sauce over the fish. Cover with a lid or foil and bake for 20 minutes in a moderately hot oven, 350 deg. F, Gas Mark 5. Remove from the oven. Have ready a serving dish bordered with cooked rice. Spoon the fish into the centre and pour over a further ¼ pint (150 ml) of curry sauce.

Garnish with lemon wedges and parsley.

N.B. This sauce is coarse or lumpy in texture, very different from the normal, smooth curry sauce. It has a mild-to-medium flavour but if you or your family prefer a hotter curry add more curry powder initially.

PUDDINGS AND SWEETS

A tremendous variety of puddings and sweets may be stored in the freezer, and for busy housewives – particularly those who have husbands and families with a sweet tooth – a supply of frozen puddings ready to cook or warm through is especially welcome on those very busy days when there is just no time to cook, or when that unexpected guest arrives. Many of the items, such as fruit pies, filled pancakes, éclairs and sponge cakes have already been dealt with in the chapter How to Freeze Home Baking (see pages 54–65) and can, with a swirl of whipped cream or a scoop of ice cream, be very quickly turned into delicious puddings. But let's now look at some of the more basic puddings which are most suitable for family meals.

Steamed fruit puddings using suet crust pastry freeze very well before or after steaming, and many of the fruits which are suitable for these you may already have in your freezer, e.g. apple slices, plums, black-currants, gooseberries, rhubarb, or any combination of these fruits. Aluminium foil basins are best for the storage of raw or pre-cooked puddings.

SUET CRUST PASTRY

Ingredients:

8 oz. (225 g) plain flour	½ teaspoon salt
4 oz. (100 g) suet (use packet suet	1 teaspoon baking powder
or finely chopped or minced suet)	About ¼ pint (150 ml) of cold water

Method: Sift flour and salt into a bowl and add the suet and rub into the flour with finger tips. Make a well in the centre and add the cold water, and with a round-bladed knife mix to an elastic consistency. Turn onto a floured board, knead until smooth and use as required.

GUIDE TO QUANTITIES AND PORTIONS

Size of basin	1 pint (600 ml)	1½ pints (¾ l.)	2 pints (1 l.)
Amount of suet pastry	4 oz. (100 g)	6 oz. (175 g)	8 oz. (225 g)
Amount of prepared fruit	6–8 oz. (175–225 g)	8 oz. (225 g)	12 oz. (350 g)
Portions	3–4	6	8

Allow 4 oz. sugar (100 g) to each pound (½ kg) of fruit.
The weight of pastry refers to the quantity of flour from which the pastry was prepared.

METHOD OF PREPARING STEAMED FRUIT PUDDINGS

Grease the basin with cooking oil.

Divide the pastry into one third for the top and two thirds for the lining.

Roll out the pastry for lining the basin to ½″ (1 cm) in thickness. Place in basin and with the finger tips mould from the centre of the base outwards until the pastry is evenly spread to the top rim.

Put half the fruit into the basin, add the sugar, then the remaining fruit. The fruit should not more than three-quarters fill the basin. Dampen the top rim with cold water.

Roll the remaining one third of pastry into a round to fit on top of the fruit. Place in position, dampen round the edge and fold the lining pastry over it. Seal well.

Cover with a circle of greaseproof paper and then cover with freezer foil.

The pudding may be frozen raw at this stage, or steamed for two hours if you wish to cook it before freezing. Then cool quickly.

The choice is yours but there are occasions when you may have time for preparation and not cooking.

To serve: Place frozen puddings in a steamer. Steam *raw pudding mixtures* for $2\frac{1}{2}$ hours and *cooked puddings* for 45 minutes.

Puddings with crumb topping freeze well in their raw state and are a good standby for school holidays and busy days. Apple, plum or rhubarb crumbles can be prepared from slightly imperfect fruits and are really enjoyed by the family during the winter months.

CRUMBLE TOPPING

Ingredients:

6 oz. (150 g) plain flour	sugar
3 oz. (75 g) soft brown or caster	4 oz. (100 g) margarine

Method: Sift flour into a bowl, add cut-up margarine and rub it into the flour until it begins to oil and the mixture sticks together. Add sugar and mix well. Use as required.

GUIDE TO QUANTITIES AND PORTIONS

Size of container	$\frac{3}{4}$ pint (40 ml)	1 pint ($\frac{1}{2}$ l.)	$1\frac{1}{2}$ pints ($\frac{3}{4}$ l.)
Weight of topping (made weight)	6 oz. (175 g)	9 oz. (250 g)	12 oz. (350 g)
Weight of prepared fruit	8 oz. (225 g)	12 oz. (350 g)	1 lb. ($\frac{1}{2}$ kg)
Portions	3–4	5–6	5–8

Allow 3 oz. (75 g) sugar to each pound ($\frac{1}{2}$ kg) of fruit.

METHOD OF PREPARING CRUMBLE TOPPED PUDDINGS

Arrange the selected fruit in a greased foil container, mixing the sugar through the fruit. Sprinkle the topping over and press down lightly. Seal, label and freeze.

To serve: Place uncooked pudding in cold oven set at 400 deg. F, Gas Mark 6, and bake for 30 minutes. Lower the heat to 375 deg. F, Gas Mark 5 and continue cooking for 25–30 minutes until the fruit is tender and the topping crisp.

N.B. Crumble topping may be prepared as suggested and, if time or freezer space is at a premium, the crumble can be packed in polythene bags and used when required.

STEAMED PUDDINGS   Using cake mixture

Puddings made from plain cake mixture, or from the recipe which I gave on page 61 for a Victoria sponge, freeze well and can be prepared in family-sized portions using foil basins or as individual puddings using dariole moulds. The puddings can be prepared and frozen raw or steamed for 1½–2 hours if to be cooked before freezing.

To serve: Place the frozen puddings into a steamer and steam *raw puddings* for about 2½ hours, and *cooked puddings* for about 45 minutes. Raw dariole moulds cook from frozen in a steamer in 45–50 minutes or, if you have the oven on, 30 minutes at 375 deg. F, Gas Mark 5.

Serve with custard or jam sauce. But my favourite to serve with a lemon or orange flavoured steamed sponge pudding is *Lemon sauce.*

LEMON SAUCE

Ingredients:

½ teacup sugar	mixed to a paste with 2 table-
1 teacup boiling water	spoons water
1 oz. (25 g) butter	Pinch salt
1 heaped tablespoon cornflour	Rind and juice of 2 lemons

Method: Put water, sugar and rind into a saucepan and bring to the boil. Remove from heat and add blended cornflour, lemon juice and butter.

Return to heat and stir constantly until the sauce boils. Reduce heat and simmer for 2 minutes.

COLD SWEETS USING GELATINE

The freezing of a table jelly is not recommended, neither is that of any other gelatine set jellies, because during freezing the ice crystals formed break up the structure of the jelly and whilst the jelly will remain set it loses its clear bright appearance and develops a coarse granular texture. However, when gelatine is used as a setting agent for creams, soufflés, etc., the granular quality of the jelly is masked and the thawed results are good. You can, therefore, use your own favourite recipe for fruit creams, cold soufflés etc., with every confidence.

Ice cream is almost a must in every freezer and no doubt you will buy a variety of flavours either in gallons or half-gallons depending on the age or the number of your family. And how useful the plastic containers can be when all the ice cream has been eaten. Ice cream is such a good standby sweet and can be served with a wide variety of other foods. A sauce is always useful to have on hand, particularly a fudge sauce which children really adore. Here is my recipe: Put into a small heavy pan 4 tablespoons soft brown sugar, 2 level tablespoons golden syrup, 1 oz. (25 g) butter and 4 tablespoons evaporated milk. Stir constantly over a low heat until all the ingredients are well blended, and simmer for 5 minutes. It is really delicious served hot or cold, poured over vanilla, chocolate or coffee ice cream. It can be frozen but it does keep well in the refrigerator. When entertaining decorate with chopped walnuts, maraschino cherries and whipped cream.

One of my favourite cold sweets which is so simple to make and yet so much enjoyed by my friends, is raspberries in strawberry cream, and all the ingredients may be taken from the freezer.

RASPBERRIES IN STRAWBERRY CREAM – 8 servings

Ingredients:

2 lbs. (1 kg) frozen raspberries $\frac{1}{2}$ pint (300 ml) strawberry purée
$\frac{3}{4}$ pint (400 ml) whipped cream

Method: Take raspberries from the freezer and allow to thaw out in the refrigerator for about 2 hours. Take strawberry purée from the freezer and allow to thaw out at room temperature for two hours. Divide the partially thawed raspberries equally between eight individual serving dishes (laying aside about twenty-four of the most perfect berries for decoration) – stemmed glasses are most suitable to use for this sweet. If raspberries have been frozen in their natural state dredge with caster sugar. If they have been frozen in dry sugar, no further sugar is required. Whip the cream and sweeten to taste.

Fold in the strawberry purée and pour over the raspberries. Decorate with raspberries and angelica leaves. Sponge finger biscuits may be served separately if liked.

As an alternative and equally delicious dessert strawberries may be served with raspberry cream.

ORANGE SORBET

Ingredients:

5 oz. (150 g) sugar $6\frac{3}{4}$ fl. oz. (175 ml) can of frozen
$\frac{3}{4}$ pint (400 ml) water   orange juice
2 egg whites

Method: Dissolve sugar in water, bring to the boil and simmer uncovered for 10 minutes. Turn the frozen orange juice, undiluted, into a bowl, and pour on the sugar syrup, stirring. When cold, pour into an ice cube tray and freeze to a mushy consistency in the freezer. Whisk egg whites until thick and foamy but not dry, and fold into the orange mush. Pile into six Tupperware parfait dishes to within 1″ ($2\frac{1}{2}$ cm) of the top, seal and freeze upright until firm. At this stage the base stands can be removed and the containers stored for up to 2 months in the freezer either upright or horizontal.

To serve: Remove seals and 'frost up' the top of each sorbet with a teaspoon.

11. Looking after your freezer

DEFROSTING AND CLEANING

A chest freezer will only require to be defrosted once, or at the most twice, a year. Ideally this should be done when food stocks are low, but by using the following method it can be done quickly and easily whether the freezer is virtually full or nearly empty. Twenty-four hours before deciding to defrost, set the controls to the fast freeze position, so that the food packed in the freezer will become as cold as possible.

Next morning, or whenever during that day you are going to defrost, switch off and remove the plug from the socket. Remove the food and pack it in strong cardboard boxes; egg boxes are most useful for this – you could collect a few from the supermarket – but if this is not possible, pack the food well together and leave in a cool place, covered with plenty of newspaper, or a blanket; both act as good insulation. Spread a bath towel on the bottom of the freezer and then place a plastic bowl or pail of hot water inside the freezer. Close the lid and leave for one hour. After that time the frost will be easily removed from the sides of the freezer – use a plastic or wooden scraper for this job. Remove the frost which falls from the sides to the bottom before the frost melts. This does save too much mopping up at the end. Leave the lid open for a further half hour or until the cabinet has completely defrosted. Remove bath towel from the bottom of the freezer, mopping up any remaining water. Wash out the inside of the cabinet with warm water in which a little bicarbonate of soda has been dissolved, then dry thoroughly. Pull out the freezer – it's easy to move when empty, but almost impossible when full – wash down the back and sides, removing any obstinate marks with a spray polish.

Return freezer to its position, plug in and switch on, leaving the control on fast freeze. Remember, if you had taped the plug initially, re-tape now – much better to be safe than sorry. You are now ready to re-pack, and while doing so take this opportunity of making sure that all packs are still correctly wrapped and labelled. Lay aside any unidentifiable packs for inspection when the re-packing has been completed.

If you keep a stock book, check the items as you return them to the freezer. Leave the fast freeze control switch on overnight and return to normal running the next day.

An upright freezer should be defrosted in the same way, but defrosting should be done three or four times in the year, or when there is a build-up of white frost to a depth of $\frac{1}{4}''$ on the freezing coils. This very much

78

depends on how often the door or doors are opened.

COPING WITH EMERGENCIES

Freezer breakdowns

Telephone your service engineer immediately the fault has been discovered. He should then be able to advise you of his expected time of arrival. Please don't panic. The food in your freezer will remain in good condition for at least twenty-four hours, but please *NEVER LIFT THE LID OR OPEN THE DOOR.*

Power failure

This could be caused by bad weather conditions causing disruption in the supply of electricity in your area, faults occurring at generating stations or national emergencies when the power is switched off for several hours to conserve supplies. This situation is usually not as serious for the freezer owner as is first imagined. In most cases power failures last only for a few hours, and remember the food in your freezer will remain in good condition for at least twenty-four hours. Again *DO NOT LIFT THE LID OR OPEN THE DOOR* and immediately the power has been restored, switch the controls to fast freeze for about six hours. If you have been advised by your local electricity board that the power failure is likely to last more than twelve hours, then for your own peace of mind and to prevent any deterioration in the food, try to make arrangements to have your food stored – your butcher may be able to help you or your frozen food supplier will help if he has cold room facilities and his own supply has not been affected. A friend in another area may be able to help you. If after twenty-four hours the supply is still off and no help is available, then the situation is very serious indeed – the food must be used up. Eat what you can and give away the remainder, but remember all the raw food in your freezer could be cooked and re-frozen. I do sincerely hope that *you* never have to cope with this emergency.

MOVING HOUSE

You always know well in advance just when you are moving house, so try to run the stock down as much as possible. It is a good idea to keep sufficient food in the freezer to see you through the first few difficult days of settling in, but please check with the removers that they will handle a partially loaded cabinet. Providing the move takes no longer than 12–14 hours, the food will remain in perfect condition. Switch the controls to fast freeze 24 hours before the move, so that the food is very cold, and as added insulation place an old blanket on top of the food – yes, freeze it too. Check *before* you move that you have a plug top suitable for the new house and that the supply will be connected for your arrival.

The freezer should be loaded last and unloaded first.

Good cooking, good freezing, and good luck, in your whole new world of Better Living.

TABLE OF INSTRUCTIONS FOR PREPARATION AND COOKING OF VEGETABLES

VEGETABLE	PREPARATION	BLANCHING TIME Cooling time in minutes
ASPARAGUS	Wash thoroughly and sort according to size. Cut stalks 4″–6″ long. Freeze less tender pieces for soups and purées.	2–4 according to thickness of stalk
BEANS (broad)	Pod and wash. Sort into sizes if necessary.	3
BEANS (French)	Trim ends. String if necessary. Wash.	2–3 according to size
BEANS (runner)	Trim ends and string. Wash, slice coarsely cutting diagonally across the bean.	2–3
BEETROOT, small whole	Not bigger than 2″ in diameter. Wash well.	25–30 or till tender (skin when blanched)
BROCCOLI	Wash and sort according to size. Remove coarse stalks. Soak in salted water for 30 minutes to remove any insects.	3
BRUSSELS SPROUTS	Select small tight ones. Remove excess leaves. Soak in salted water for 30 minutes to remove any insects.	3
CABBAGE	Usually in plentiful supply but freeze if you have a good garden crop. Discard coarse outer leaves. Cut into wedges. Soak in salted water for 30 minutes to remove any insects.	3–4
CABBAGE (shredded)	Discard coarse outer leaves. Shred. Soak in salted water for 30 minutes to remove any insects.	$1–1\frac{1}{2}$

PACKING	STORAGE TIME	COOKING TIME From frozen
Whole spears head to tail in waxed cartons or Tupperware containers.	8–12 months	7–10 minutes
Polythene bags	8–12 months	8–10 minutes
Polythene bags	8–12 months	7–8 minutes
Polythene bags	8–12 months	5–6 minutes
Polythene bags for whole beetroot, freezer containers for sliced and diced.	8–12 months	Already cooked; warm through or serve in vinegar.
Waxed containers or boxes lined with waxed paper. Tupperware containers. Pack alternately head to tail.	8–12 months	10–12 minutes
Polythene bags	8–12 months	8–10 minutes
Polythene bags	8–12 months	In boiling salted water. 10–15 minutes.
Polythene bags	8–12 months	8–10 minutes

VEGETABLE	PREPARATION	BLANCHING TIME Cooling time in minutes
CARROTS	Wash thoroughly and scrape. Leave small ones whole. Dice or slice others.	5 (small whole) 3 (diced or sliced)
CAULIFLOWER	Trim leaves and break heads into florets. Let stand in salted water until ready to blanch. Separate small and large pieces for blanching.	3 (small) 4 (large)
CELERY	Scrub stalks and top and tail. Cut into even-sized pieces.	3
CORN-ON-THE-COB	Husk – remove silk carefully. Separate cobs into equal sizes for blanching.	4–6 N.B. After blanching kernels may be remov from cob. Pack in bag – takes up less freezer
COURGETTES	Wash. Cut in half or into slices. Can be sautéed in butter, cooled and frozen.	1–2
MUSHROOMS AND FIELD MUSHROOMS	Peel – remove stalk. Sauté in butter. Freeze on trays.	Do not blanch
MUSHROOM STALKS	Slice firm stalks. Sauté in butter.	Do not blanch
PEAS	Use young tender peas. Pod and sort by size.	Small – 1 Large – 2
PEPPERS (green and red)	Wash. Remove seeds and stems. Cut in half. Slice or dice according to use.	Not necessary for short-term storage. Long-term storage – 2 minutes.
POTATOES (new)	Choose small even-sized ones and scrape.	Blanch until almost cooked. Drain and cool.

PACKING	STORAGE TIME	COOKING TIME From frozen
Polythene bags	8–12 months	10–15 minutes Small whole 10 minutes, diced or sliced.
Polythene bags	8–12 months	10–15 minutes
Polythene bags. Can only be used as cooked vegetable – when frozen loses its crispness.	8–12 months	8–10 minutes
Polythene bags. Individually wrapped in freezer film.	8–12 months	5–10 minutes. Must be allowed to thaw before cooking to avoid a cold core.
Polythene bags or freezer containers.	6 months	5–7 minutes Warm through if sautéed in butter.
Polythene bags or containers.	6 months	Fry or grill
Polythene bags	6 months	Use for soups or casseroles.
Polythene bags	8–12 months	5–7 minutes
Polythene bags or cartons.	6–8 months	Can be used in salads if unblanched. Add to casseroles etc. without thawing.
Polythene bags or 'Boil in the Bag'. If packed in a 'Boil in the Bag' add a tablespoon of water and a tablespoon of butter and a sprig of mint before freezing.	8–12 months	Can be gently heated in a little salted water with mint and butter.

VEGETABLE	PREPARATION	BLANCHING TIME Cooking time in minutes
POTATOES (chips)	Cut chips and soak for ½ hour. Drain and dry.	Fry in oil until almost cooked but not coloured.
POTATOES (mashed)	Cook and mash potatoes in normal way. Make into croquettes or Duchesse potatoes.	Open freeze on trays
SPINACH	Wash very thoroughly. Remove thick stems.	2–3
TOMATOES (whole)	Choose firm ripe tomatoes. Remove skin if liked, but this is not necessary.	No blanching
TOMATO PURÉE	Choose ripe tomatoes, blanch and peel. Rub through a sieve or liquidize and strain.	½–1
Root Vegetables: SWEDES TURNIPS PARSNIPS	Wash. Peel, dice or cut into slices about ½″ thick. Can also be fully cooked and mashed with butter.	Diced – 1 Cut – 2
VEGETABLE PURÉES	Cook vegetables in boiling water until soft. Rub through sieve or liquidize.	
Herbs: PARSLEY, THYME, ROSEMARY, SAGE, MINT (chopped)	Prepare, wash and chop.	No blanching
HERBS (whole)	Wash and shake dry.	No blanching
VEGETABLES (mixed)	Prepare, blanch and cool each variety according to directions given.	

PACKING	STORAGE TIME	COOKING TIME From frozen
Open freeze on trays. Pack in bags.	4–6 months	Partially thaw and deep fry.
Containers Tupperware	6–8 months	Warm through
Pack tightly in polythene bags. Use a square-type container as a mould.	8–12 months	4–6 minutes. *Very* little water.
Open freeze. Pack into containers or polythene bags.	8–12 months	Use for frying, grilling or adding to casseroles. *Not suitable* for using raw. Can also be used for chutney.
Pack in glass jars or con- tainers. Leave head space for expansion.	8–12 months	Use in soup, sauces or casseroles.
Polythene bags, Tupperware or in container lined with polythene bag. Freeze and remove bag.	8–12 months	15–20 minutes. Warm through.
Glass jars or containers. Allow head space for expansion.	8–12 months	Useful for soups and baby foods.
Ice cube trays. When frozen store in polythene bags or tiny containers.	8–12 months	Use cubes direct in soups, sauces etc.
Polythene bags.	8–12 months	Crumbled between the fingers give a chopped effect.
Mix before packing in polythene bags.	8–12 months	Most useful for soups and stews.

TABLE OF INSTRUCTIONS FOR PREPARATION AND COOKING OF FRUIT

FRUIT	PREPARATION
APPLES (purée)	Peel and core. Windfalls are ideal for purée.
APPLES (slices)	Peel, core and slice into salted water to prevent browning.
BLACKBERRIES BRAMBLES	Wash only if necessary.
BLACKCURRANTS REDCURRANTS	Pick over to remove any damaged fruit. Do not wash unless absolutely necessary.
CHERRIES	Wash and dry. Remove stones if to be kept frozen for more than six months.
GOOSEBERRIES	Wash and dry, top and tail.
MELON	Must be ripe. Do *not* freeze in slices. Cut into cubes or shape into balls.
PEACHES	If possible peel without blanching or blanch in boiling water for not longer than one minute. Cool immediately in iced water. Remove skin, cut in half and remove stones. Slice if desired.
PEARS	Peel and core. Halve or slice and place in salted water – submerged until you have prepared sufficient for poaching.
PLUMS (all varieties) DAMSONS GREENGAGES	Wash and dry. Remove stones if fruit is being stored for more than six months.

PACKING	SUGGESTIONS FOR USE
Cook with minimum amount of water. Beat to a pulp and sweeten to taste. Pack in small quantities in containers.	Heat from frozen for sauce or thaw in containers either in refrigerator or at room temperature.
Blanch in boiling water for 2 minutes and cool. Pack with or without sugar in containers.	For puddings, pies or tarts, thaw enough to separate slices. For stewing cook from frozen.
Methods 1 or 3 (see page 43). Pack in containers.	Thaw in unopened containers in refrigerator. For stewing cook from frozen. Ideal for mixing with apples.
Method 3 (see page 44). Stalks should be removed after freezing by gentle rubbing. Pack in containers for table use, in bags for jam and jelly.	For stewing cook from frozen. For jam and jelly cook from frozen.
Method 2 (see page 44) is recommended, but method 1 can be used. Pack in containers.	To serve raw, thaw in unopened containers and use while still frosty. For stewing, cook from frozen in own syrup if method 2 is used.
Method 1 or 3 (see page 43). Pack in bags.	Partially thaw before using in pies and tarts. For stewing cook from frozen in the minimum amount of water. Excellent for chutney.
Method 2 (see page 44). Pack in containers.	Thaw in container in refrigerator. Eat while still frosty.
Method 2 (see page 44). Fruit must be submerged immediately in syrup.	Thaw in refrigerator in unopened containers.
Poach in sugar syrup for 2 minutes. Cool. Fruit must be submerged in syrup.	Thaw in refrigerator in unopened containers.
Method 2 (see page 44) for all light coloured plums and greengages. Dark coloured plums can be frozen by Method 3 (see page 44).	For stewing cook from frozen in own syrup. Plums frozen by method 3 can be used for tarts and pies.

FRUIT	PREPARATION
RASPBERRIES	Pick over carefully. Do not wash unless absolutely necessary.
RHUBARB	Wash and trim. Cut diagonally into 1″ lengths (2½ cm).
STRAWBERRIES	Hull and remove any damaged berries. Do not wash unless absolutely necessary.
Citrus fruits: ORANGES LEMONS GRAPEFRUITS	Although these fruits are readily available throughout the year, they can be frozen when the price is low. Good quality ripe fruit can be frozen whole, but whole fruit frozen does not look very attractive, although the juice when the fruit has thawed out is of good quality. As juice, in segments, with or without sugar, but sugar does improve the flavour. Rinds can be grated. The half fruits normally discarded after squeezing can be wrapped in film and frozen and used as shells for sorbets or water ices. Slices of lemon frozen by method 3 are most useful to have in the freezer for drinks or for a refreshing cup of lemon tea.
MARMALADE ORANGES	This fruit has a very short season so make full use of your freezer. Scrub and thoroughly dry the fruit – open freeze whole fruit and pack in bags. Use frozen for whole fruit recipes or thaw until soft enough for squeezing and slicing. Remember to add 10% extra weight of fruit for pectin loss for your favourite recipe.

PACKING	SUGGESTIONS FOR USE
Use methods 1, 2, or 3 (see page 43).	Thaw in unopened containers in refrigerator. If frozen by methods 1 or 3, thaw and eat if possible while still frosty.
Method 1 or 3 (see page 43).	Partially thaw for pies. Cook from frozen for stewing. Do not add any water. Stew gently.
Method 1 or 3; method 4 for imperfect or damaged berries (see page 44).	Thaw in unopened containers. Best served when still frosty.

Shopping in your local frozen food shop

With more and more families becoming freezer owners the demand for commercially frozen foods is increasing rapidly, and throughout the country the increase in the number of shops specializing in offering this service is phenomenal. Although many of us do a certain amount of food freezing at home, there are very few freezer owners who do not buy frozen goods. In fact I would say that the home freezer is not really completely stocked without them. The advantages of this type of shopping are tremendous, and the two main savings are money and time. Your personal needs and where you live, whether in the country or in the town, and whether you enjoy cooking or not, will determine what you buy.

Frozen vegetables and fruit

The selection these days is excellent and frozen vegetables are always in demand, from the ever-popular garden peas to the courgettes and peppers. Fruit is always a good buy if you have not frozen your own, and the choice is wide. There is now never an out-of-season fruit, as every frozen food shop can usually offer a wide variety from rhubarb to fruit salad. When comparing prices of frozen fruits and vegetables with fresh, the most important point to take into consideration is that with the frozen fruits and vegetables, everything in the bag or packet can be used – there is absolutely no waste, and no doubt as to freshness, as commercially frozen food is always harvested at the peak of its condition, and the time taken from harvesting to freezing is very short indeed. Many families almost look upon as necessities frozen chips, fish fingers, beef-burgers, sausages, pies and sausage rolls, Cornish pasties etc. The ready to bake range of pies and pastry savouries are always very popular, especially when the quality is just as good as you can make yourself.

Fish is also a worthwhile buy and it can be purchased already prepared, ready to cook. Prepared fish such as egged and crumbed cod, haddock, plaice or sole, should always be cooked from frozen. The manufacturers normally give cooking instructions on the packet. All varieties of white fish are also available in fillets or cutlets, usually in a shatter pack, so that you are able to use the number of fillets or weight required for a specific recipe. Smoked fish and kippers too are a worthwhile buy for the freezer. Frozen poultry is always available and bags of chicken quarters or pieces. The pizza pie is popular, as are pasta dishes and Chinese foods. You can serve a wide variety of interesting dishes to your family and your friends with the help of your freezer and your local frozen food shop. Here are a few recipes using some of these commercially prepared foods which I hope you will try. They are all easily prepared and I hope your family will enjoy them.

STUFFED HAMBURGERS   Serves 4

Ingredients:

4 2 oz. (50 g) frozen hamburgers
2 large onions, sliced, or
4 oz. (100 g) frozen sliced onions

2 tomatoes, sliced
8 rashers streaky bacon

Method: Allow the hamburgers to thaw and flatten, using a round bladed knife or rolling pin. Fry the sliced onion, cooking gently until golden brown. On one half of each hamburger place fried onions and sliced tomato, season with salt and pepper. Fold over, pressing the edges well together. Wrap two rashers of bacon, well stretched with a round-bladed knife, round each one, and fry until brown on both sides. Reduce heat and cook for a further 10 minutes.

Serve in warmed buttered soft rolls or, if liked, with a green salad. This is a really delicious savoury – ideal for a snack lunch or late supper.

N.B.   Beefburgers may be used in this recipe if liked.

FISHERMAN'S PIE   Serves 4

Ingredients:

1½ lbs. (¾ kg) frozen white fish (cod,
   (haddock, whiting or saithe)
1 10½ oz. can condensed tomato soup
1 oz. (25 g) plain flour mixed to a paste

with 4 tablespoons cold water
8 oz. (225 g) frozen peas
1 lb. (½ kg) mashed potatoes (potato
   powder may be used)

Method: Poach the fish in water for 8–10 minutes depending on thickness of fillets. Strain off liquid *reserving ¼ pint*. Mix the flour paste with the fish liquor and the tomato soup. Bring slowly to the boil, stirring constantly. Add flaked fish and peas.

Place this mixture in a 2 pint ovenproof dish and cover with mashed potato.

N.B.   The quickest and easiest method of doing this is using a large piping bag and a No. 8 star nozzle. Dot with butter and cook in a moderately hot oven, 400 deg. F. Gas Mark 6, for 25 minutes.

Serve if liked, with sliced green beans or any vegetable of your own choosing.

CRUNCHIE SAUSAGE ROLLS

Ingredients:

8 thin slices of white bread
4 oz. (100 g) grated cheese
2 oz. (50 g) table margarine
1 level teaspoon made mustard

½ level teaspoon salt
8 frozen skinless beef or pork
   sausages
Wooden cocktail sticks

Method: Remove crusts from bread and roll out lightly to make each slice thinner. Cream together the margarine, cheese, mustard and salt. Spread this mixture on the bread – place a sausage on each slice and roll up. Cut each roll in half and secure with a *wooden* cocktail stick. Place on a well-greased tray and bake in a moderately hot oven, 400 deg. F. Gas Mark 6, for 25–30 minutes until golden brown and crisp. Serve hot.

N.B.   These rolls may be prepared in advance if you wish to serve them when entertaining. Over-wrap the tray with film or foil and store in the refrigerator. The sausages will then have thawed out and the cooking time should be reduced by 10 minutes.

Another great favourite which I serve, really by popular demand, is:

PIGS IN CHEESY BLANKETS

Ingredients:

8 frozen skinless beef or pork sausages
4 oz. (100 g) self-raising flour
¼ teaspoon salt
1 oz. (25 g) vegetable fat shortening

3 oz. (75 g) finely grated cheese
4 tablespoons cold water
Wooden cocktail sticks
Cooking oil for deep frying

Method: Fry or grill the frozen sausages until cooked and allow to cool. Place all the ingredients for the pastry, including the cheese, in a bowl. Mix to a soft dough with a fork. Turn out on to a floured board and knead until smooth. Roll out to ⅛″ in thickness and cut into 3″ squares. Cut each sausage in half and lay diagonally across the pastry square. Fold two corners diagonally across the sausage and secure with a *wooden* cocktail stick.
Deep fry in oil until golden brown.

These savouries are always very popular – allow at least two if not three per person. Please remember to use *wooden* cocktail sticks. You won't believe this but there are the housewives who have used *plastic* ones – need I say more!

And now, for that special occasion when you would like to serve something different, why not try –

GAMMON STEAKS WITH GINGER SNAP SAUCE   Serves 4

Ingredients:

4 5 oz. (150 g) gammon steaks
8 small peach halves
2 oz. (50 g) finely chopped walnuts

1 teaspoon dry mustard
½ teacup soft brown sugar

Ginger Snap Sauce

Ingredients:

4 ginger snap biscuits
¼ teacup vinegar
1 teacup water

½ teacup seedless raisins
Juice of one lemon

Method: Allow the gammon steaks to thaw in the refrigerator overnight.

92

Mix sugar, mustard and chopped walnuts together and add enough peach juice to bind and form a soft paste. Place gammon steaks brushed with melted lard or oil on the grid of grill pan. Cook for 5–8 minutes on either side, depending on thickness. Turn frequently, then spread mustard mixture evenly over the steaks. Fill the peach halves with brown sugar. Place steaks and peach halves under the grill and cook on a medium heat for a further 5–8 minutes. Care must be taken at this stage to prevent the spread from over-browning.

Ginger Snap Sauce

Method: Crush the ginger snaps either in your blender or place in a polythene bag and crush with rolling pin. Place crumbs in saucepan and add all the other ingredients.

Bring slowly to boiling point, stirring constantly.

Reduce heat and simmer for 5 minutes.

Serve steaks with sauce poured over.

Garnish with caramelised peaches and parsley or watercress, accompanied by boiled potatoes, sweet corn and green vegetables of your own choosing.

A tossed green salad may also be served.

And as a starter:

MELON AND GREEN FIG COCKTAIL   Serves 8

Ingredients:

2 lb. (1 kg) packet of frozen melon balls	3 oz. (75 g) stem ginger
1 tin green figs	$\frac{1}{4}$ pint (150 ml) ginger syrup

Method: Allow the melon balls to thaw out overnight in the refrigerator. Drain off liquid. Place melon balls in a bowl and add quartered green figs plus the syrup from the can, chopped stem ginger and ginger syrup. Mix well together and return to the refrigerator for at least two hours before serving in individual glasses.

Decorate, if liked, with a thin twist of orange or lemon peel.

N.B.   I discard the syrup from the melon balls as it does tend to weaken the delicate and unusual flavour of this cocktail.

It goes against the grain for me to waste anything, but honestly I have never been able to find a suitable use for it.

Other items which you will find when shopping for frozen foods include mouth watering cold sweets such as rum babas, chocolate eclairs, cheesecakes and gâteaux, and although these are fairly expensive the quality is excellent and so much enjoyed on that special occasion. Remember too, all the luxury ice cream products and water ices.

Index